The Unofficial

Tik Tok

CookBook

#2023

150 viral Fan Favorite Delicious and Healthy recipes for Ice-cream, Snacks, Drinks, Treats, BBQ And More.

Susan Siler

TABLE OF CONTENT

INTRODUCTION

Welcome to the exciting world of TikTok, where culinary trends go viral and creativity has no boundaries. This book is for you if you've ever found yourself browsing through your TikTok feed as your mouth waters over amazing culinary creations. The most well-liked and well-known dishes that have taken TikTok by storm are collected in the charming The Unofficial TikTok Cookbook. This cookbook is your entry point for re-creating the enchantment of TikTok in your own kitchen with tantalizing viral food trends, creative hacks, and fast meal ideas. TikTok has completely changed the way we share and consume material, and this extends to the food industry as well. TikTok has grown to be a platform for food lovers and aspiring cooks to share their culinary experiences and display their delectable products because of its snappy videos and fascinating narration. We have collected an enticing collection of dishes from throughout the world that have won the hearts and taste buds of millions. You may discover everything in these pages, from fluffy pancake cereal and whipped coffee to delectable baked feta spaghetti and the newest cuisine craze. Behind-the-scenes information, inventive methods, and insider knowledge that can help you master these TikTok hits have been revealed. Step-by-step directions, eye-catching pictures, and helpful hints are included with every recipe to help you succeed in the kitchen. This cookbook offers something for everyone, whether you're a TikTok enthusiast ready to imitate your favorite culinary trends or just searching for ideas to spice up your meals. It honors the happiness, originality, and sense of community that TikTok provides to the world of cooking. So put on your apron, switch on your favorite TikTok music, and come along for an unforgettable culinary journey with us. Prepare to explore a world of tastes, pamper your senses, and experience the magic of TikTok in the comfort of your own home. The Unofficial TikTok Cookbook aims to thrill your taste buds, inspire you, and keep you entertained. Let's start a meal!

A special Burger

Servings: 4

Nutrition: 994 Calories,

42g Carbohydrates, 39g Protein, 73g Fat

Ingredients:

- ✓ 2 Tbsp. minced onion
- ✓ ¾ cup mayo
- ✓ 2 Tbsp. apple cider vinegar
- ✓ 2 Tbsp. sugar
- ✓ ½ tsp. celery seed
- ✓ 1 packet chili seasoning
- ✓ 1 cup water
- ✓ ½ small sweet onion minced
- ✓ 1 16 oz package coleslaw mix
- ✓ ¼ tsp. garlic powder
- ✓ ¼ tsp. pepper
- ✓ ¼ tsp. salt
- ✓ 1 pound ground beef
- ✓ ½ cup ketchup
- ✓ 4 bakery buns
- ✓ 2 Tbsp. yellow mustard
- ✓ 2 Tbsp. diced onions for topping
- ✓ ½ pound ground chuck (85%)
- ✓ 1 tsp. steak seasoning
- ✓ 4 slices cheddar cheese

Directions:

1. In order to prepare the slaw, put all of the ingredients in a large mixing bowl and chill until needed.
2. On a griddle over medium heat, brown the ground beef before adding the chilli spice, water, onion, and ketchup. Grill the meat and chilli for 10 minutes, or until the flesh is soft. Pat the ground

chuck into four equal (thin) patties, then top with burger-specific steak seasoning. Cooking should continue until everything is done. Cheddar cheese should be heated until melted.

3. Before constructing the burgers, spread yellow mustard inside the buns. On the bottom bread, place the hamburger patty. On top, add slaw, onions, and chilli. Lastly, add a top bun. By inserting a steak knife through the top bread, you can hold the burger together.
4. Add more chilli and creamy sauces to the side when serving your burgers.

Yummy Toast with Strawberries

Servings: 4

Nutrition: 508 Calories,

91g Carbohydrates, 11g Protein, 10g Fat

Ingredients:
- ✓ 1 Cup Maple Syrup
- ✓ 8 Strawberries
- ✓ 8 Slices Bread
- ✓ 4 Tabelspoons Butter
- ✓ 1 Tablespoon Powdered Sugar
- ✓ 1 Tabelspoon Cinnamon
- ✓ ½ Teaspoon Nutmeg
- ✓ 1 Tablespoon Sugar
- ✓ 4 Eggs
- ✓ ½ Tablespoon Vanilla extract

Directions:

1. Put all of the ingredients in a large mixing dish and refrigerate until required to make the slaw.
2. Brown the ground beef on a griddle over medium heat before adding the ketchup, onion, water, and chilli powder. For 10

minutes, or until the flesh is tender, grill the pork and chilli. The ground chuck should be formed into four equal, thin patties before being seasoned for burgers.

3. Cooking needs to go on until everything is prepared. The cheddar cheese has to be warmed up until it melts. Spread mustard on the buns before assembling the burgers. Place the hamburger patty on the bottom slice of bread. Add slaw, onions, and chilli on top.

4. Add a top bun last. You may hold the burger together by slicing through the top bread with a steak knife.

5. When serving your burgers, put more creamy and chilli sauces on the side.

Mouth-watering caramelized Apple Pancakes

Servings: 4

Nutrition: 486 Calories,

77g Carbohydrates, 10g Protein, 16g Fat

Ingredients:

- ✓ 1 medium apple peeled and grated
- ✓ Butter or cooking spray for cooking the pancakes
- ✓ 2 pinches of salt
- ✓ 1 cup milk
- ✓ 4 tablespoons butter melted
- ✓ 2 eggs beaten
- ✓ 1 1/2 cups all-purpose flour
- ✓ 2 tablespoons sugar
- ✓ 2 teaspoons baking powder
- ✓ 1 teaspoon baking soda
- ✓ ¼ teaspoon ground cinnamon
- ✓ 2 apples peeled, core, diced
- ✓ 2 tablespoons brown sugar
- ✓ 2-3 tablespoons caramel sauce
- ✓ ½ teaspoon vanilla extract

Directions:

1. To create the slaw, combine all the ingredients in a large mixing bowl and chill until needed.
2. On a griddle over medium heat, sear the ground beef before adding the ketchup, onion, water, and chilli powder.
3. Grill the pork and chilli for 10 minutes, or until the meat is soft. Before seasoning the ground chuck for burgers, it should be divided into four equal, thin patties. The cooking must continue until everything is ready.
4. It is necessary to reheat the cheddar cheese until it melts. Before constructing the burgers, spread mustard on the buns. Put the hamburger patty on the bread's bottom slice. On top, sprinkle slaw, onions, and chilli. Last, add the top bun. By cutting through the top bread with a steak knife, you can keep the burger from falling apart.
5. More creamy and spicy sauces should be served on the side while serving the burgers.

Delicious Monkey Bread with Cookies

Servings: 4

Nutrition: 250 Calories,

10g Fat, 40g Carbohydrates, 2g Protein

Ingredients:

- ✓ Sugar, Granulated 1/2 cup
- ✓ Cinnamon, Ground. 1 tablespoon
- ✓ Biscuits, Grands 1 can
- ✓ Butter, Melted 2 tablespoons

Directions:

1. Combine all the ingredients for the slaw in a large mixing bowl and refrigerate until required.

2. Sear the ground beef on a griddle over medium heat before adding the ketchup, onion, water, and chilli powder. For 10 minutes, or until the meat is tender, grill the pork and chilli. The ground chuck should be split into four equal, thin patties before seasoning the burgers.
3. Until everything is done, the cooking must go on. The cheddar cheese must be heated until it melts. Spread mustard on the buns before assembling the burgers. Place the bottom piece of bread with the hamburger patty on it. Sprinkle slaw, onions, and chilli powder on top.
4. Add the top bun last. You can prevent the burger from coming apart by using a steak knife to cut through the top slice of bread.
5. The burgers should be served with more sour cream and hot sauce on the side.

Chicken Breast with Asian flavors

Servings: 4

Nutrition: 321 Calories,

14g Carbohydrates, 48g Protein, 7g Fat

Ingredients:

- ✓ 2 tablespoon soy sauce
- ✓ 1 teaspoon sesame oil
- ✓ 1 teaspoon sriracha
- ✓ 1 tablespoon ginger paste
- ✓ 4 chicken breasts sliced into tenders
- ✓ 3 tablespoon honey

Directions:

1. In a large mixing bowl, combine all the slaw ingredients. Refrigerate until needed.
2. On a griddle over medium heat, sear the ground beef before adding the ketchup, onion, water, and chilli powder. Grill the pork and chilli for 10 minutes, or until the flesh is tender. Before

seasoning the burgers, the ground chuck should be divided into four equal, thin patties.

3. The cooking must continue until everything is finished. It is necessary to cook the cheddar cheese until it melts. Before constructing the burgers, spread mustard on the buns. Put the hamburger patty on the bottom piece of bread. On top, sprinkle slaw, onions, and chilli powder.

4. Lastly, add the top bun. By slicing through the top piece of bread with a steak knife, you can keep the burger from falling apart.

5. More sour cream and spicy sauce need to be offered alongside the burgers.

Buffalo Chicken Tortillas

Servings: 16

Nutrition: 510 Calories,

39g Carbohydrates, 33g Protein, 24g Fat

Ingredients:

- ✓ 1 Tbs. Water
- ✓ 1 Tbs. Cornstarch
- ✓ 4 oz. Cream Cheese
- ✓ 1 ¼ lbs. Boneless skinless Chicken Breasts
- ✓ 3 Tbs. Frank's Red Hot Buffalo Wing Sauce
- ✓ ½ cup Honey
- ✓ ½ tsp Chili Powder
- ✓ ½ tsp Ground Cumin
- ✓ ¼ tsp White Pepper
- ✓ ¼ cup Brown Sugar
- ✓ 2 Tbs. Soy Sauce
- ✓ 1 tsp Salt
- ✓ 1 tsp Garlic Powder
- ✓ ½ tsp Onion Powder
- ✓ 1 tsp Smoked Paprika
- ✓ Sour cream

- ✓ 1 Large Tomato Diced
- ✓ Olive Oil
- ✓ Guacamole
- ✓ 1 (16 oz) bag of Fiesta or Mexican blend shredded cheese
- ✓ 3 (12 oz) packages of Street Taco Mini Flour Tortillas

Directions:

1. All the slaw ingredients should be combined in a large mixing dish. Keep chilled until required. Sear the ground beef on a griddle over medium heat before adding the ketchup, onion, water, and chilli powder.
2. For 10 minutes, or until the meat is soft, grill the pork and chilies. The ground chuck should be split into four equal, thin patties before seasoning the burgers. Until everything is done, the cooking must continue.
3. The cheddar cheese must be heated until it melts. Spread mustard on the buns before assembling the burgers. On the bottom piece of bread, place the hamburger patty. Add slaw, onions, and chilli powder over top. \
4. Add the top bun last. You can prevent the burger from crumbling by using a steak knife to cut through the top slice of bread. The burgers should be served with more sour cream and hot sauce.

Asian Chicken Fried Rice

Servings: 6

Nutrition: 670 Calories,

30g Carbohydrates, 25g Protein, 50g Fat

Ingredients:

- ✓ 3 tablespoons soy sauce
- ✓ 3 large eggs
- ✓ 2 cups white rice
- ✓ 1 small onion, chopped
- ✓ 2 teaspoons garlic powder

- ✓ 1 tablespoon sesame seed oil
- ✓ 1 pound chicken tenderloins
- ✓ 8 ounces (1/2 pound) bacon
- ✓ 3 tablespoons butter
- ✓ 3 cups chopped vegetables

Directions:

1. In a large mixing bowl, combine all the slaw ingredients. Refrigerate until needed.
2. On a griddle over medium heat, sear the ground beef before adding the ketchup, onion, water, and chilli powder.
3. Grill the pork and the chilies for 10 minutes, or until the flesh is tender. Before seasoning the burgers, the ground chuck should be divided into four equal, thin patties. The cooking must go on until everything is finished. It is necessary to cook the cheddar cheese until it melts. Before constructing the burgers, spread mustard on the buns.
4. The hamburger patty should be placed on the bottom slice of bread.
5. On top, sprinkle slaw, onions, and chilli powder. Lastly, add the top bun.
6. By slicing through the top piece of bread with a steak knife, you can stop the burger from collapsing. More sour cream and spicy sauce need to be added to the burgers' servings.

Quick and easy turkey and cheese sandwiches

Servings: 1

Nutrition: 950 Calories,

57g Fat, 78g Carbohydrates, 36g Protein

Ingredients:

- ✓ 2 Tablespoons pesto
- ✓ 1 small tomato, sliced
- ✓ 1 1/2 slices Havarti cheese

- ✓ 3 slices oven-roasted turkey
- ✓ 2 slices sourdough bread
- ✓ 2 Tablespoons butter softened

Directions:

1. All the slaw ingredients should be combined in a large mixing dish. Keep chilled until required. Sear the ground beef on a griddle over medium heat before adding the ketchup, onion, water, and chilli powder.
2. For 10 minutes, or until the meat is soft, grill the pork and the chilies. The ground chuck should be split into four equal, thin patties before seasoning the burgers. Until everything is done, the cooking must continue. The cheddar cheese must be heated until it melts. Spread mustard on the buns before assembling the burgers.
3. On the bottom piece of bread, put the hamburger patty. Add slaw, onions, and chilli powder over top. Add the top bun last. You can prevent the burger from collapsing by using a steak knife to cut through the top slice of bread.
4. The portions of the burgers require more sour cream and hot sauce.

Tasty grilled Salmon

Servings: 4

Nutrition: 631 Calories,

2g Carbohydrates, 81g Protein, 31g Fat

Ingredients:

- ✓ 1 tsp garlic salt
- ✓ 1/2 tsp crushed red pepper
- ✓ 1 tsp parsley
- ✓ 1 1/2 tbsp olive oil extra virgin
- ✓ 1/8 tsp black pepper
- ✓ 1/2 tsp white sugar

- ✓ 1 Filet Salmon
- ✓ 1 tsp lemon zest
- ✓ 1 tsp basil

Directions:

1. In a large mixing bowl, combine all the slaw ingredients. Refrigerate until needed. On a griddle over medium heat, sear the ground beef before adding the ketchup, onion, water, and chilli powder.
2. Grill the pork and the chilies for 10 minutes, or until the flesh is tender. Before seasoning the burgers, the ground chuck should be divided into four equal, thin patties. The cooking must go on until everything is finished. It is necessary to cook the cheddar cheese until it melts. Before constructing the burgers, spread mustard on the buns.
3. Place the hamburger patty on the bread slice at the bottom. On top, sprinkle slaw, onions, and chilli powder. Lastly, add the top bun.
4. By slicing through the top piece of bread with a steak knife, you can stop the burger from collapsing. The burger amounts call for extra sour cream and spicy sauce.

Rock star Burgers

Servings: 6

Nutrition: 638 Calories,

45g Carbohydrates, 49g Protein, 28g Fat

Ingredients:

- ✓ 6 Buns
- ✓ 1 tbsp Butter
- ✓ 6 slices American Cheddar
- ✓ 1 lbs Top Sirloin
- ✓ 1 tbsp Kosher Salt
- ✓ 0.5 lbs Brisket

- ✓ 1/4 cup Ketchup
- ✓ 2 tbsp Mustard
- ✓ 1/2 cup Mayonnaise
- ✓ 1 tsp Franks Hot Sauce
- ✓ 1 Dill Pickle

Directions:

1. All the slaw ingredients should be combined in a large mixing dish. Keep chilled until required. Sear the ground beef on a griddle over medium heat before adding the ketchup, onion, water, and chilli powder.
2. For 10 minutes, or until the meat is soft, grill the pork and the chilies. The ground chuck should be split into four equal, thin patties before seasoning the burgers. Until everything is done, the cooking must continue. The cheddar cheese must be heated until it melts. Spread mustard on the buns before assembling the burgers.
3. On the bottom piece of bread, place the hamburger patty. Add slaw, onions, and chilli powder over top. Add the top bun last. You can prevent the burger from collapsing by using a steak knife to cut through the top slice of bread.
4. Extra sour cream and spicy sauce are required for the burger serving sizes.

Tasty Mexican birria Tacos

Servings: 8

Nutrition: 366 Calories,

6g Carbohydrates, 34g Protein, 23g Fat

Ingredients:

- ✓ ½ teaspoon dried marjoram
- ✓ ¼ teaspoon ground cloves
- ✓ ¼ cup apple cider vinegar
- ✓ 1 -2 teaspoons chicken or beef bouillon

- ✓ 2 tablespoons olive oil
- ✓ Salt and ground black pepper to taste
- ✓ 6 dried Guajillo peppers
- ✓ 3 dried Ancho chiles
- ✓ 1 large tomato
- ✓ 3 to 4 pounds beef chuck cut into large chunks about 3-inch pieces
- ✓ 1 small cinnamon stick
- ✓ 2 bay leaves
- ✓ 1 large onion peeled and slice into thick rounds
- ✓ 6 garlic cloves peeled
- ✓ 1 teaspoon black peppercorns
- ✓ 2 teaspoons dried oregano
- ✓ 2 teaspoons ground cumin
- ✓ Canola oil or non-stick cooking spray to grease the griddle.
- ✓ Corn tortillas
- ✓ Chopped onions
- ✓ Chopped cilantro
- ✓ Any mild melting Mexican cheese
- ✓ Lime wedges

Directions:

1. In a large mixing bowl, combine all the slaw ingredients. Refrigerate until needed. On a griddle over medium heat, sear the ground beef before adding the ketchup, onion, water, and chilli powder. Grill the pork and the chilies for 10 minutes, or until the flesh is tender.
2. Before seasoning the burgers, the ground chuck should be divided into four equal, thin patties. The cooking must go on until everything is finished.
3. It is necessary to cook the cheddar cheese until it melts. Before constructing the burgers, spread mustard on the buns. The hamburger patty should be placed on the bottom slice of bread.

On top, sprinkle slaw, onions, and chilli powder. Lastly, add the top bun.

4. By slicing through the top piece of bread with a steak knife, you can stop the burger from collapsing. For the burger serving sizes, more sour cream and hot sauce are needed.

Traditional Cheesesteak on the griddle

Servings: 4

Nutrition: 476 Calories,

26g Fat, 35g Carbohydrates, 25g Protein

Ingredients:

- ✓ 1/2 cup cheez whiz or slices of favorite cheese
- ✓ salt & pepper to taste
- ✓ butter
- ✓ 1 medium onion
- ✓ 1 bell pepper
- ✓ 1 pound sliced steak
- ✓ 4 rolls

Directions:

1. All the slaw ingredients should be combined in a large mixing dish.
2. Keep chilled until required. Sear the ground beef on a griddle over medium heat before adding the ketchup, onion, water, and chilli powder. For 10 minutes, or until the meat is soft, grill the pork and the chilies.
3. The ground chuck should be split into four equal, thin patties before seasoning the burgers. Until everything is done, the cooking must continue. The cheddar cheese must be heated until it melts.
4. Spread mustard on the buns before assembling the burgers. On the bottom piece of bread, put the hamburger patty. Add slaw, onions, and chilli powder over top. Add the top bun last. You can

prevent the burger from collapsing by using a steak knife to cut through the top slice of bread.

5. More sour cream and spicy sauce are required to accommodate the burger serving sizes.

Delicious Brussels Sprouts with crispy Bacon

Servings: 6

Nutrition: 56 Calories,

6g Carbohydrates, 2g Protein, 3g Fat

Ingredients:

- ✓ 1 tablespoon olive oil
- ✓ ½ teaspoon salt
- ✓ ½ teaspoon pepper
- ✓ 2 shallots
- ✓ ½ teaspoon garlic powder
- ✓ 3 cups Brussel sprouts trimmed, loose leaves removed, and halved
- ✓ 6 slices bacon chopped

Directions:

1. In a large mixing bowl, combine all the slaw ingredients. Refrigerate until needed. On a griddle over medium heat, sear the ground beef before adding the ketchup, onion, water, and chilli powder.
2. Grill the pork and the chilies for 10 minutes, or until the flesh is tender.
3. Before seasoning the burgers, the ground chuck should be divided into four equal, thin patties. The cooking must go on until everything is finished. It is necessary to cook the cheddar cheese until it melts. Before constructing the burgers, spread mustard on the buns.

4. Place the hamburger patty on the bread slice at the bottom. On top, sprinkle slaw, onions, and chilli powder. Lastly, add the top bun.
5. By slicing through the top piece of bread with a steak knife, you can stop the burger from collapsing.
6. To account for the number of burger servings, add more sour cream and hot sauce.

Traditional Cheesesteak on the griddle

Servings: 4

Nutrition: 476 Calories,

26g Fat, 35g Carbohydrates, 25g Protein

Ingredients:

- ✓ 1/2 cup cheez whiz or slices of favorite cheese
- ✓ salt & pepper to taste
- ✓ butter
- ✓ 1 medium onion
- ✓ 1 bell pepper
- ✓ 1-pound sliced steak
- ✓ 4 rolls

Directions:

1. All the slaw ingredients should be combined in a large mixing dish. Keep chilled until required.
2. Sear the ground beef on a griddle over medium heat before adding the ketchup, onion, water, and chilli powder.
3. For 10 minutes, or until the meat is soft, grill the pork and the chilies. The ground chuck should be split into four equal, thin patties before seasoning the burgers. Until everything is done, the cooking must continue. The cheddar cheese must be heated until it melts. Spread mustard on the buns before assembling the burgers. On the bottom piece of bread, place the hamburger patty.

4. Add slaw, onions, and chilli powder over top. Add the top bun last. You can prevent the burger from collapsing by using a steak knife to cut through the top slice of bread.
5. Additional sour cream and spicy sauce should be added to adjust for the number of burgers served.

Pepperoni flavored Sandwiches Pizza

Servings: 4

Nutrition: 424 Calories,

27g Carbohydrates, 17g Protein, 28g Fat

Ingredients:

- ✓ ½ teaspoon garlic powder
- ✓ ½ teaspoon italian seasoning
- ✓ ½ cup italian gravy
- ✓ 4 tablespoons unsalted butter
- ✓ 1 ⅓ cup shredded mozzarella cheese
- ✓ ½ cup mini pepperoni slices
- ✓ 8 slices white bread

Directions:

1. In a large mixing bowl, combine all the slaw ingredients. Refrigerate until needed. On a griddle over medium heat, sear the ground beef before adding the ketchup, onion, water, and chilli powder.
2. Grill the pork and the chilies for 10 minutes, or until the flesh is tender.
3. Before seasoning the burgers, the ground chuck should be divided into four equal, thin patties. The cooking must go on until everything is finished. It is necessary to cook the cheddar cheese until it melts.
4. Before constructing the burgers, spread mustard on the buns. The hamburger patty should be placed on the bottom slice of bread.

5. On top, sprinkle slaw, onions, and chilli powder. Lastly, add the top bun. By slicing through the top piece of bread with a steak knife, you can stop the burger from collapsing.
6. To account for the quantity of burgers served, more sour cream and hot sauce should be added.

Tuna and Spinach Sandwiches

Servings: 2

Nutrition: 448 Calories,

20g Carbohydrates, 15g Protein, 34g Fat

Ingredients:

- ✓ 3 tablespoons Mayonnaise
- ✓ 1 tablespoon Mustard
- ✓ 2 tablespoons sweet pickle, diced about 1 small pickle
- ✓ 2 tablespoons butter
- ✓ 1 cup fresh baby spinach, packed and diced
- ✓ 8 slices very thin sharp cheddar cheese
- ✓ 1 5.4 oz can Albacore Tuna
- ✓ 4-6 slices white Sandwich Bread

Directions:

1. All the slaw ingredients should be combined in a large mixing dish. Keep chilled until required.
2. Sear the ground beef on a griddle over medium heat before adding the ketchup, onion, water, and chilli powder.
3. For 10 minutes, or until the meat is soft, grill the pork and the chilies. The ground chuck should be split into four equal, thin patties before seasoning the burgers. Until everything is done, the cooking must continue. The cheddar cheese must be heated until it melts. Spread mustard on the buns before assembling the burgers.
4. On the bottom piece of bread, put the hamburger patty. Add slaw, onions, and chilli powder over top. Add the top bun last.

You can prevent the burger from collapsing by using a steak knife to cut through the top slice of bread.

5. More sour cream and spicy sauce should be added to make up for the number of burgers that were provided.

Yummy Steak Sandwich

Servings: 2

Nutrition: 527 Calories,

35g Carbohydrates, 34g Protein, 25g Fat

Ingredients:

- ✓ Half of a medium onion thinly sliced
- ✓ 4.5-ounce cooked steak
- ✓ 2 teaspoons olive oil, divided
- ✓ 3 Tablespoons horseradish aioli
- ✓ 4 slices crusty bread
- ✓ Butter
- ✓ 1.5 ounce cheese

Directions:

1. In a large mixing bowl, combine all the slaw ingredients. Refrigerate until needed.
2. On a griddle over medium heat, sear the ground beef before adding the ketchup, onion, water, and chilli powder. Grill the pork and the chilies for 10 minutes, or until the flesh is tender.
3. Before seasoning the burgers, the ground chuck should be divided into four equal, thin patties. The cooking must go on until everything is finished. It is necessary to cook the cheddar cheese until it melts.
4. Before constructing the burgers, spread mustard on the buns.
5. Place the hamburger patty on the bread slice at the bottom. On top, sprinkle slaw, onions, and chilli powder. Lastly, add the top bun.

6. By slicing through the top piece of bread with a steak knife, you can stop the burger from collapsing. To compensate for the lack of burgers, more sour cream and hot sauce should be added.

Greek Sandwiches with Chicken and Cheese

Servings: 4

Nutrition: 605 Calories,

36g Fat, 27g Carbohydrates, 41g Protein

Ingredients:

- ✓ 1/4 teaspoon pepper
- ✓ 3 garlic cloves, minced
- ✓ 1 tablespoon plus 1/4 cup olive oil, divided
- ✓ 1-pound boneless skinless chicken breasts, cubed
- ✓ 1/4 teaspoon kosher salt
- ✓ 1/2 cup fresh mint leaves, chopped
- ✓ 2 tablespoons minced fresh oregano
- ✓ 2 tablespoons capers, drained
- ✓ 6 ounces fresh mozzarella cheese, shredded
- ✓ 8 slices olive or Italian bread
- ✓ 1/2 cup crumbled feta cheese
- ✓ 1/2 cup grated Parmesan cheese

Directions:

1. All the slaw ingredients should be combined in a large mixing dish.
2. Keep chilled until required. Sear the ground beef on a griddle over medium heat before adding the ketchup, onion, water, and chilli powder.
3. For 10 minutes, or until the meat is soft, grill the pork and the chilies. The ground chuck should be split into four equal, thin patties before seasoning the burgers. Until everything is done, the cooking must continue. The cheddar cheese must be heated until it melts.

4. Spread mustard on the buns before assembling the burgers. On the bottom piece of bread, place the hamburger patty. Add slaw, onions, and chilli powder over top.
5. Add the top bun last. You can prevent the burger from collapsing by using a steak knife to cut through the top slice of bread.
6. There should be more sour cream and spicy sauce added to make up for the absence of hamburgers.

Spicy chili Hot Dogs

Servings: 8

Nutrition: 492 Calories,

26g Carbohydrates, 24g Protein, 32g Fat

Ingredients:

- ✓ 1 cup shredded cheddar cheese
- ✓ 1 tablespoon olive oil
- ✓ 1 large white onion, diced
- ✓ 8 all beef hot dogs
- ✓ 8 hotdog buns
- ✓ 1 (14.5-ounce) can tomatoes, diced, or crushed
- ✓ 2 tablespoons mustard
- ✓ ¼ cup water
- ✓ 1 jalapeno, diced
- ✓ 2 teaspoons ground cumin
- ✓ 1 tablespoon garlic powder
- ✓ 1 tablespoon chili powder
- ✓ ¼ cup ketchup
- ✓ Salt and pepper, to taste
- ✓ Vegetable oil, for the griddle
- ✓ 1 ½ pounds ground beef
- ✓ 1 white onion, diced

Directions:

1. In a large mixing bowl, combine all the slaw ingredients. Refrigerate until needed.
2. On a griddle over medium heat, sear the ground beef before adding the ketchup, onion, water, and chilli powder. Grill the pork and the chilies for 10 minutes, or until the flesh is tender. Before seasoning the burgers, the ground chuck should be divided into four equal, thin patties.
3. The cooking must go on until everything is finished. It is necessary to cook the cheddar cheese until it melts. Before constructing the burgers, spread mustard on the buns.
4. The hamburger patty should be placed on the bottom slice of bread. On top, sprinkle slaw, onions, and chilli powder. Lastly, add the top bun.
5. By slicing through the top piece of bread with a steak knife, you can stop the burger from collapsing.
6. To make up for the lack of hamburgers, additional sour cream and spicy sauce should be added.

Delicious fried Chicken

Servings: 4

Nutrition: 383 Calories,

24g Carbohydrates, 29g Protein, 18g Fat

Ingredients:
- ✓ 1 egg
- ✓ 1 cup flour
- ✓ 2/3 tsp salt
- ✓ 1 lb boneless skinless chicken breasts
- ✓ 4 tbsp oil
- ✓ 1/4 tsp pepper

Directions:

1. All the slaw ingredients should be combined in a large mixing dish. Keep chilled until required. Sear the ground beef on a

griddle over medium heat before adding the ketchup, onion, water, and chilli powder.

2. For 10 minutes, or until the meat is soft, grill the pork and the chilies.

3. The ground chuck should be split into four equal, thin patties before seasoning the burgers. Until everything is done, the cooking must continue. The cheddar cheese must be heated until it melts. Spread mustard on the buns before assembling the burgers.

4. On the bottom piece of bread, put the hamburger patty. Add slaw, onions, and chilli powder over top. Add the top bun last.

5. You can prevent the burger from collapsing by using a steak knife to cut through the top slice of bread.

6. Add more sour cream and hot sauce to compensate for the absence of hamburgers.

Pizza with Sausage and Mushrooms

Servings: 2

Nutrition: 1082 Calories,

70g Fat, 72g Carbohydrates, 45g Protein

Ingredients:

- ✓ 6 ounces ground Italian sausage, hot or mild
- ✓ 1/2 cup prepared pesto
- ✓ 2 cups diced mushrooms, any type
- ✓ 2 Flatbread Crusts
- ✓ 1 cup shredded Mozzarella cheese
- ✓ 1/2 cup sauteed onions

Directions:

1. In a large mixing bowl, combine all the slaw ingredients. Refrigerate until needed.

2. On a griddle over medium heat, sear the ground beef before adding the ketchup, onion, water, and chilli powder.
3. Grill the pork and the chilies for 10 minutes, or until the flesh is tender. Before seasoning the burgers, the ground chuck should be divided into four equal, thin patties. The cooking must go on until everything is finished. It is necessary to cook the cheddar cheese until it melts.
4. Before constructing the burgers, spread mustard on the buns. Place the hamburger patty on the bread slice at the bottom. On top, sprinkle slaw, onions, and chilli powder.
5. Lastly, add the top bun. By slicing through the top piece of bread with a steak knife, you can stop the burger from collapsing.
6. To make up for the lack of hamburgers, increase the amount of sour cream and spicy sauce.

Delicious Omelette with Mushrooms and Ham

Servings: 1

Nutrition: 372 Calories,

24g Fat, 4g Carbohydrates, 35g Protein

Ingredients:
- ✓ Mushrooms, Diced Small 1/4 cup
- ✓ Ham, Sliced Thin, Diced Small 1/3 cup
- ✓ Egg, Large 2 each
- ✓ Cheese, Colby Jack, Shredded. 1/3 cup

Directions:

1. All the slaw ingredients should be combined in a large mixing dish.
2. Keep chilled until required. Sear the ground beef on a griddle over medium heat before adding the ketchup, onion, water, and chilli powder. For 10 minutes, or until the meat is soft, grill the pork and the chilies.

3. The ground chuck should be split into four equal, thin patties before seasoning the burgers. Until everything is done, the cooking must continue. The cheddar cheese must be heated until it melts.
4. Spread mustard on the buns before assembling the burgers. On the bottom piece of bread, place the hamburger patty. Add slaw, onions, and chilli powder over top.
5. Add the top bun last. You can prevent the burger from collapsing by using a steak knife to cut through the top slice of bread.
6. Increase the sour cream and spicy sauce to make up for the absence of hamburgers.

Italian Pizza on the griddle

Servings: 12

Nutrition: 271 Calories,

15g Fat, 22g Carbohydrates, 12g Protein

Ingredients:

- ✓ Pizza Sauce 1 cup
- ✓ Shredded Cheese 4 cups
- ✓ Pizza Dough Kit 18 oz
- ✓ Toppings - Assortment

Directions:

1. In a large mixing bowl, combine all the slaw ingredients. Refrigerate until needed.
2. On a griddle over medium heat, sear the ground beef before adding the ketchup, onion, water, and chilli powder. Grill the pork and the chilies for 10 minutes, or until the flesh is tender.
3. Before seasoning the burgers, the ground chuck should be divided into four equal, thin patties. The cooking must go on until everything is finished. It is necessary to cook the cheddar cheese until it melts.

4. Before constructing the burgers, spread mustard on the buns. The hamburger patty should be placed on the bottom slice of bread.
5. On top, sprinkle slaw, onions, and chilli powder. Lastly, add the top bun.
6. By slicing through the top piece of bread with a steak knife, you can stop the burger from collapsing. To make up for the lack of hamburgers, add more sour cream and hot sauce.

Chicken Wings with BBQ sauce

Servings: 6

Nutrition: 804 Calories,

58g Fat, 32g Carbohydrates, 39g Protein

Ingredients:

- ✓ Salt 1/2 teaspoon
- ✓ Pepper 1/4 teaspoon
- ✓ Sweet Baby Ray's BBQ Sauce 1/2 cup
- ✓ Chicken Wings 3 Pounds
- ✓ Drakes Frymix 3/4 cup
- ✓ Oil for frying

Directions:

1. All the slaw ingredients should be combined in a large mixing dish. Keep chilled until required. Sear the ground beef on a griddle over medium heat before adding the ketchup, onion, water, and chilli powder.
2. For 10 minutes, or until the meat is soft, grill the pork and the chilies.
3. The ground chuck should be split into four equal, thin patties before seasoning the burgers. Until everything is done, the cooking must continue. The cheddar cheese must be heated

until it melts. Spread mustard on the buns before assembling the burgers.

4. On the bottom piece of bread, put the hamburger patty. Add slaw, onions, and chilli powder over top. Add the top bun last. You can prevent the burger from collapsing by using a steak

5. knife to cut through the top slice of bread. Add additional sour cream and spicy sauce to compensate for the absence of hamburgers

Tasty Crab cake

Servings: 5

Nutrition: 151 Calories,

5g Fat, 17g Carbohydrates, 10g Protein

Ingredients:

✓ Breadcrumbs, Italian 3/4 cup
✓ Mushroom 1/2 cup
✓ Egg 1 each
✓ Salt 1/2 teaspoon
✓ Crab Meat, White 6 ounce
✓ Butternut Squash, Shredded 1 cup
✓ Pepper 1/4 teaspoon
✓ Olive Oil 1 tablespoon

Directions:

1. In a large mixing bowl, combine all the slaw ingredients. Refrigerate until needed.
2. On a griddle over medium heat, sear the ground beef before adding the ketchup, onion, water, and chilli powder.
3. Grill the pork and the chilies for 10 minutes, or until the flesh is tender. Before seasoning the burgers, the ground chuck should be divided into four equal, thin patties. The cooking must go on

until everything is finished. It is necessary to cook the cheddar cheese until it melts.

4. Before constructing the burgers, spread mustard on the buns. Place the hamburger patty on the bread slice at the bottom. On top, sprinkle slaw, onions, and chilli powder. Lastly, add the top bun.
5. By slicing through the top piece of bread with a steak knife, you can stop the burger from collapsing.
6. To make up for the lack of hamburgers, increase the sour cream and hot sauce.

Traditional American fried Chicken Wings

Servings: 6

Nutrition: 764 Calories,

57g Fat, 22g Carbohydrates, 38g Protein

Ingredients:
- ✓ Drakes Frymix 3/4 cup
- ✓ Salt 1/2 teaspoon
- ✓ Chicken Wings 3 Pounds
- ✓ Pepper 1/4 teaspoon
- ✓ Oil for frying

Directions:

1. All the slaw ingredients should be combined in a large mixing dish.
2. Keep chilled until required. Sear the ground beef on a griddle over medium heat before adding the ketchup, onion, water, and chilli powder. For 10 minutes, or until the meat is soft, grill the pork and the chilies.
3. The ground chuck should be split into four equal, thin patties before seasoning the burgers. Until everything is done, the cooking must continue. The cheddar cheese must be heated until it melts.

4. Spread mustard on the buns before assembling the burgers. On the bottom piece of bread, place the hamburger patty. Add slaw, onions, and chilli powder over top.
5. Add the top bun last. You can prevent the burger from collapsing by using a steak knife to cut through the top slice of bread.
6. Increase the sour cream and spicy sauce to make up for the absence of hamburgers.

Noodles with smoked Beef

Servings: 10

Nutrition: 284 Calories,

11g Fat, 18g Carbohydrates, 28g Protein

Ingredients:

- ✓ 16 ounces rice vermicelli noodles
- ✓ 1 tablespoon of beef rub
- ✓ 2 pounds whole beef sirloin roast
- ✓ 2 whole carrots
- ✓ 2 green onions
- ✓ 8 ounces green cabbage
- ✓ 1 tablespoon sugar
- ✓ 1/2 teaspoon black pepper
- ✓ 1/4 cup soy sauce
- ✓ 1 cup beef stock

Directions:

1. In a large mixing bowl, combine all the slaw ingredients. Refrigerate until needed.
2. On a griddle over medium heat, sear the ground beef before adding the ketchup, onion, water, and chilli powder. Grill the pork and the chilies for 10 minutes, or until the flesh is tender. Before seasoning the burgers, the ground chuck should be divided into four equal, thin patties.

3. The cooking must go on until everything is finished. It is necessary to cook the cheddar cheese until it melts.
4. Before constructing the burgers, spread mustard on the buns. The hamburger patty should be placed on the bottom slice of bread.
5. On top, sprinkle slaw, onions, and chilli powder. Lastly, add the top bun.
6. By slicing through the top piece of bread with a steak knife, you can stop the burger from collapsing.
7. To make up for the lack of hamburgers, add more sour cream and hot sauce.

Gourmet Steak on your griddle

Servings: 1

Nutrition: 600 Calories,

2g Fat, 5g Carbohydrates, 25g Protein

Ingredients:

- ✓ 1 steak
- ✓ salt
- ✓ pepper
- ✓ vegetables to taste

Directions:

1. All the slaw ingredients should be combined in a large mixing dish.
2. Keep chilled until required. Sear the ground beef on a griddle over medium heat before adding the ketchup, onion, water, and chilli powder.
3. For 10 minutes, or until the meat is soft, grill the pork and the chilies.
4. The ground chuck should be split into four equal, thin patties before seasoning the burgers. Until everything is done, the

cooking must continue. The cheddar cheese must be heated until it melts. Spread mustard on the buns before assembling the burgers.

5. On the bottom piece of bread, put the hamburger patty. Add slaw, onions, and chilli powder over top. Add the top bun last.
6. You can prevent the burger from collapsing by using a steak knife to cut through the top slice of bread.
7. Add additional sour cream and spicy sauce to compensate for the absence of hamburgers.

Delicious Steak served with Egg on top

Servings: 1

Nutrition: 843 Calories,

62g Fat, 2g Carbohydrates, 66g Protein

Ingredients:

- ✓ Salt 1/4 teaspoon
- ✓ Pepper 1/8 teaspoon
- ✓ Herb Garlic Butter. 2 teaspoons
- ✓ Steak 8 ounces
- ✓ Olive Oil 1 teaspoon
- ✓ Egg 1 each

Directions:

1. In a large mixing bowl, combine all the slaw ingredients. Refrigerate until needed.
2. On a griddle over medium heat, sear the ground beef before adding the ketchup, onion, water, and chilli powder. Grill the pork and the chilies for 10 minutes, or until the flesh is tender.
3. Before seasoning the burgers, the ground chuck should be divided into four equal, thin patties.
4. The cooking must go on until everything is finished.

5. It is necessary to cook the cheddar cheese until it melts. Before constructing the burgers, spread mustard on the buns. Place the hamburger patty on the bread slice at the bottom. On top, sprinkle slaw, onions, and chilli powder. Lastly, add the top bun.
6. By slicing through the top piece of bread with a steak knife, you can stop the burger from collapsing.
7. To make up for the lack of hamburgers, increase the sour cream and hot sauce.

Garlic butter flavored Steak

Servings: 1

Nutrition: 771 Calories,

57g Fat, 1g Carbohydrates, 60g Protein

Ingredients:

- ✓ Salt 1/4 teaspoon
- ✓ Pepper 1/8 teaspoon
- ✓ Steak 8 ounces
- ✓ Olive Oil 1 teaspoon
- ✓ Herb Garlic Butter. 2 teaspoons

Directions:

1. All the slaw ingredients should be combined in a large mixing dish.
2. Keep chilled until required. Sear the ground beef on a griddle over medium heat before adding the ketchup, onion, water, and chilli powder.
3. For 10 minutes, or until the meat is soft, grill the pork and the chilies.
4. The ground chuck should be split into four equal, thin patties before seasoning the burgers. Until everything is done, the cooking must continue. The cheddar cheese must be heated

until it melts. Spread mustard on the buns before assembling the burgers.

5. On the bottom piece of bread, place the hamburger patty. Add slaw, onions, and chilli powder over top. Add the top bun last.

6. You can prevent the burger from collapsing by using a steak knife to cut through the top slice of bread.

7. Increase the sour cream and spicy sauce to make up for the absence of hamburgers.

Super tasty Runza Sandwich with Beef and Vegetables

Servings: 6

Nutrition: 535 Calories,

32g Fat, 34g Carbohydrates, 28g Protein

Ingredients:

- ✓ 1/2 teaspoon seasoning salt
- ✓ 1 pound ground beef (80/20 blend)
- ✓ 1/2 teaspoon salt
- ✓ 1/2 teaspoon pepper
- ✓ 1/2 teaspoon garlic powder
- ✓ 6 slices American cheese
- ✓ 1 tube crescent roll dough sheet
- ✓ 2 tablespoons butter
- ✓ 6 cups shredded cabbage
- ✓ 1 large onion, sliced
- ✓ 1/2 teaspoon onion powder

Directions:

1. In a large mixing bowl, combine all the slaw ingredients. Refrigerate until needed. On a griddle over medium heat, sear the ground beef before adding the ketchup, onion, water, and chilli powder.

2. Grill the pork and the chilies for 10 minutes, or until the flesh is tender.
3. Before seasoning the burgers, the ground chuck should be divided into four equal, thin patties. The cooking must go on until everything is finished. It is necessary to cook the cheddar cheese until it melts. Before constructing the burgers, spread mustard on the buns.
4. The hamburger patty should be placed on the bottom slice of bread.
5. On top, sprinkle slaw, onions, and chilli powder. Lastly, add the top bun. By slicing through the top piece of bread with a steak knife, you can stop the burger from collapsing.
6. To make up for the lack of hamburgers, add more sour cream and hot sauce.

Mini Sandwiches with Mushrooms

Servings: 8

Nutrition: 345 Calories,

16g Fat, 25g Carbohydrates, 23g Protein

Ingredients:

- ✓ American Cheese, Slices 8 each
- ✓ Burger Buns, Mini 8 each
- ✓ Ground Beef. 1 pound

Directions:

1. All the slaw ingredients should be combined in a large mixing dish. Keep chilled until required. Sear the ground beef on a griddle over medium heat before adding the ketchup, onion, water, and chilli powder.
2. For 10 minutes, or until the meat is soft, grill the pork and the chilies. The ground chuck should be split into four equal, thin patties before seasoning the burgers. Until everything is done,

the cooking must continue. The cheddar cheese must be heated until it melts. Spread mustard on the buns before assembling the burgers.

3. On the bottom piece of bread, put the hamburger patty. Add slaw, onions, and chilli powder over top. Add the top bun last.
4. You can prevent the burger from collapsing by using a steak knife to cut through the top slice of bread.
5. Add additional sour cream and spicy sauce to compensate for the absence of hamburgers.

Gourmet marinated Chicken Breast

Servings: 1

Nutrition: 420 Calories,

42g Fat, 17g Carbohydrates, 106g Protein

Ingredients:

- ✓ Veggies to taste
- ✓ Chicken Breast, Boneless, Skinless. 12 oz
- ✓ Italian Dressing 5 oz

Directions:

1. In a large mixing bowl, combine all the slaw ingredients. Refrigerate until needed.
2. On a griddle over medium heat, sear the ground beef before adding the ketchup, onion, water, and chilli powder. Grill the pork and the chilies for 10 minutes, or until the flesh is tender.
3. Before seasoning the burgers, the ground chuck should be divided into four equal, thin patties. The cooking must go on until everything is finished. It is necessary to cook the cheddar cheese until it melts.
4. Before constructing the burgers, spread mustard on the buns. Place the hamburger patty on the bread slice at the bottom.

5. On top, sprinkle slaw, onions, and chilli powder. Lastly, add the top bun.
6. By slicing through the top piece of bread with a steak knife, you can stop the burger from collapsing. To make up for the lack of hamburgers, increase the sour cream and hot sauce.

Super tasty Potatoes with Cheese and Bacon

Servings: 9

Nutrition: 249 Calories,

17g Fat, 18g Carbohydrates, 7g Protein

Ingredients:

- ✓ Olive Oil 4 tablespoons
- ✓ Butter 4 tablespoons
- ✓ Simply Three Seasoning. 1 teaspoon
- ✓ Potatoes, Baby 1 1/2 pounds
- ✓ Salt 1 teaspoon
- ✓ Cheese, Shredded 1 cup
- ✓ Bacon Bits 1/2 cup

Directions:

1. All the slaw ingredients should be combined in a large mixing dish.
2. Keep chilled until required. Sear the ground beef on a griddle over medium heat before adding the ketchup, onion, water, and chilli powder.
3. For 10 minutes, or until the meat is soft, grill the pork and the chilies. The ground chuck should be split into four equal, thin patties before seasoning the burgers. Until everything is done, the cooking must continue.
4. The cheddar cheese must be heated until it melts. Spread mustard on the buns before assembling the burgers. On the bottom piece of bread, place the hamburger patty.

5. Add slaw, onions, and chilli powder over top. Add the top bun last. You can prevent the burger from collapsing by using a steak knife to cut through the top slice of bread.
6. Increase the sour cream and spicy sauce to make up for the absence of hamburgers.

Delicious Mini Pizzas

Servings: 8

Nutrition: 242 Calories,

9g Fat, 32g Carbohydrates, 8g Protein

Ingredients:

- ✓ Pizza Sauce 1/2 cup
- ✓ Shredded Cheese 1 cups
- ✓ Pillsbury Mini Pizza Crust 1 can
- ✓ Toppings

Directions:

1. In a large mixing bowl, combine all the slaw ingredients. Refrigerate until needed.
2. On a griddle over medium heat, sear the ground beef before adding the ketchup, onion, water, and chilli powder.
3. Grill the pork and the chilies for 10 minutes, or until the flesh is tender. Before seasoning the burgers, the ground chuck should be divided into four equal, thin patties. The cooking must go on until everything is finished.
4. It is necessary to cook the cheddar cheese until it melts. Before constructing the burgers, spread mustard on the buns. The hamburger patty should be placed on the bottom slice of bread.
5. On top, sprinkle slaw, onions, and chilli powder. Lastly, add the top bun. By slicing through the top piece of bread with a steak knife, you can stop the burger from collapsing.
6.

7. To compensate for the lack of hamburgers, add more sour cream and hot sauce.

Scrambled Egg Sandwich

Servings: 2

Nutrition: 272 Calories,

19g Fat, 16g Carbohydrates, 9g Protein

Ingredients:

- ✓ Mayo 1 tablespoon
- ✓ Butter 1 tablespoon
- ✓ Eggs, Large 2 each
- ✓ Bread, Slices 2 each
- ✓ Oil 1 teaspoon

Directions:

1. All the slaw ingredients should be combined in a large mixing dish.
2. Keep chilled until required. Sear the ground beef on a griddle over medium heat before adding the ketchup, onion, water, and chilli powder. For 10 minutes, or until the meat is soft, grill the pork and the chilies. The ground chuck should be split into four equal, thin patties before seasoning the burgers. Until everything is done, the cooking must continue. The cheddar cheese must be heated until it melts.
3. Spread mustard on the buns before assembling the burgers. On the bottom piece of bread, put the hamburger patty. Add slaw, onions, and chilli powder over top.
4. Add the top bun last. You can prevent the burger from collapsing by using a steak knife to cut through the top slice of bread.
5. Add additional sour cream and spicy sauce to make up for the absence of hamburgers.

Grilled Pork and Cheese Sandwich

Servings: 1

Nutrition: 494 Calories,

25g Fat, 47g Carbohydrates, 19g Protein

Ingredients:

- ✓ Cheddar Cheese, Slice 1 each
- ✓ Pulled Pork 2 oz
- ✓ Butter 1 Tablespoon
- ✓ Bread, Sliced 2 each
- ✓ BBQ Sauce 1 Tablespoon

Directions:

1. In a large mixing bowl, combine all the slaw ingredients. Refrigerate until needed.
2. On a griddle over medium heat, sear the ground beef before adding the ketchup, onion, water, and chilli powder. Grill the pork and the chilies for 10 minutes, or until the flesh is tender. Before seasoning the burgers, the ground chuck should be divided into four equal, thin patties. The cooking must go on until everything is finished.
3. It is necessary to cook the cheddar cheese until it melts. Before constructing the burgers, spread mustard on the buns. Place the hamburger patty on the bread slice at the bottom. On top, sprinkle slaw, onions, and chilli powder.
4. Lastly, add the top bun. By slicing through the top piece of bread with a steak knife, you can stop the burger from collapsing.
5. To compensate for the lack of hamburgers, add more sour cream and hot sauce.

Griddle Steak Tacos

Servings: 8

Nutrition: 703 Calories,

46g Fat, 4g Carbohydrates, 63g Protein

Ingredients:

- ✓ 1 teaspoon salt
- ✓ 1/2 teaspoon pepper
- ✓ 1/2 teaspoon garlic powder
- ✓ 1 tablespoon chile lime rub
- ✓ corn tortillas
- ✓ 4 pounds beef skirt steak
- ✓ 2 limes, juiced
- ✓ 1 small white onion, finely diced
- ✓ 1 bunch cilantro, chopped
- ✓ hot sauce of your choosing

Directions:

1. All the slaw ingredients should be combined in a large mixing dish. Keep chilled until required.
2. Sear the ground beef on a griddle over medium heat before adding the ketchup, onion, water, and chilli powder. For 10 minutes, or until the meat is soft, grill the pork and the chilies.
3. The ground chuck should be split into four equal, thin patties before seasoning the burgers. Until everything is done, the cooking must continue. The cheddar cheese must be heated until it melts.
4. Spread mustard on the buns before assembling the burgers. On the bottom piece of bread, place the hamburger patty. Add slaw, onions, and chilli powder over top.
5. Add the top bun last. You can prevent the burger from collapsing by using a steak knife to cut through the top slice of bread.
6. Add additional sour cream and spicy sauce to make up for the absence of hamburgers.

French style Sandwich

Servings: 6

Nutrition: 944 Calories,

50g Fat, 53g Carbohydrates, 71g Protein

Ingredients:

- ✓ 12 pieces of white bread
- ✓ 2 tablespoons mayo
- ✓ 2 tablespoons mustard
- ✓ 18 thin slices swiss or gruyere cheese
- ✓ 4 eggs
- ✓ 1/3 cup half and half
- ✓ powdered sugar
- ✓ raspberry jam
- ✓ 2 pounds deli thin-sliced ham

Directions:

1. In a large mixing bowl, combine all the slaw ingredients. Refrigerate until needed.
2. On a griddle over medium heat, sear the ground beef before adding the ketchup, onion, water, and chilli powder. Grill the pork and the chilies for 10 minutes, or until the flesh is tender.
3. Before seasoning the burgers, the ground chuck should be divided into four equal, thin patties. The cooking must go on until everything is finished.
4. It is necessary to cook the cheddar cheese until it melts. Before constructing the burgers, spread mustard on the buns. The hamburger patty should be placed on the bottom slice of bread.
5. On top, sprinkle slaw, onions, and chilli powder. Lastly, add the top bun. By slicing through the top piece of bread with a steak knife, you can stop the burger from collapsing.
6. To compensate for the lack of hamburgers, add more sour cream and hot sauce.

Caramelized Bananas

Servings: 6
Cooking Time: x

Ingredients:

- ✓ 10 small ripe firm bananas, peeled, chopped into chunks
- ✓ 4 whole cloves
- ✓ 4 sticks cinnamon
- ✓ 2 cups brown sugar
- ✓ Whipped cream or vanilla ice cream to serve

Directions:

1. All the slaw ingredients should be combined in a large mixing dish. Keep chilled until required. Sear the ground beef on a griddle over medium heat before adding the ketchup, onion, water, and chilli powder.
2. For 10 minutes, or until the meat is soft, grill the pork and the chilies.
3. The ground chuck should be split into four equal, thin patties before seasoning the burgers. Until everything is done, the cooking must continue. The cheddar cheese must be heated until it melts. Spread mustard on the buns before assembling the burgers.
4. On the bottom piece of bread, put the hamburger patty. Add slaw, onions, and chilli powder over top. Add the top bun last. You can prevent the burger from collapsing by using a steak knife to cut through the top slice of bread.
5. Add additional sour cream and spicy sauce to make up for the absence of hamburgers.

Mulled Wine (1)

Servings: x
Cooking Time: 1 Hour

Ingredients:

- ✓ 2 oranges, thinly sliced
- ✓ 2 cups apple cider
- ✓ 1 bottle full bodied red wine
- ✓ 1 cup orange juice
- ✓ ¼ Cup honey
- ✓ 2 cinnamon sticks
- ✓ 1 tsp. whole allspice
- ✓ 1 tsp. whole cloves

Directions:

1. In a large mixing bowl, combine all the slaw ingredients. Refrigerate until needed.
2. On a griddle over medium heat, sear the ground beef before adding the ketchup, onion, water, and chilli powder. Grill the pork and the chilies for 10 minutes, or until the flesh is tender. Before seasoning the burgers, the ground chuck should be divided into four equal, thin patties.
3. The cooking must go on until everything is finished. It is necessary to cook the cheddar cheese until it melts. Before constructing the burgers, spread mustard on the buns. Place the hamburger patty on the bread slice at the bottom.
4. On top, sprinkle slaw, onions, and chilli powder. Lastly, add the top bun.
5. By slicing through the top piece of bread with a steak knife, you can stop the burger from collapsing.
6. To compensate for the lack of hamburgers, add more sour cream and hot sauce.

Eggnog

Servings:x
Cooking Time:x

Ingredients:

- ✓ 4 Egg Yolks
- ✓ 8 Eggs
- ✓ 4 cups Milk
- ✓ 3 cups Heavy Cream
- ✓ 1 Vanilla bean
- ✓ 1 cup Powdered Sugar
- ✓ 1/2 tsp. Salt
- ✓ 2 Cinnamon Sticks
- ✓ 1/2 tsp. Clove
- ✓ 1/2 A Whole Nutmeg, Grated
- ✓ 2 cups Bourbon
- ✓ Equipment
- ✓ 4 32oz mason jars

Directions:

1. 144 degrees Fahrenheit ought to be the temperature of the water bath.
2. Blend the milk, heavy cream, sugar, cloves, egg yolks, whole eggs, milk, and heavy cream until smooth. Blend the vanilla after removing it from the bean. Peels from vanilla beans should be kept. Add one-half of a grated nutmeg. Half a cinnamon stick and a quarter of a vanilla pod should be added to each jar. Blend the mixture until frothy.
3. Four 32-ounce canning jars should be full. Make sure the bourbon is dispersed evenly after adding a little to the jars. Jars for canning should be finger-tight but not unduly so. Cook the jars in a water bath for an hour. Once you're done, just put it in the fridge for the night.
4. Although it is excellent to consume straight away, ageing it for an additional week will help to mellow down the alcohol flavour.
5. Add some freshly grated nutmeg on top, then serve.

Sriracha Turkey Bites

Preparation time: 10 minutes

Cooking time: 2 hours

Servings: 4

Ingredients:
- ✓ 2 lb. turkey breast, skinless, boneless and cubed
- ✓ 1 tbsp. olive oil
- ✓ 1 tbsp. soy sauce
- ✓ 2 tbsp. tomato sauce
- ✓ 2 tsp. sriracha sauce
- ✓ ¼ cup chives, chopped
- ✓ ½ tsp. chili powder
- ✓ Salt and black pepper to the taste

Directions:

1. To prepare this appetiser, combine the turkey, oil, sriracha sauce, and the other ingredients in a sous vide bag, mix to combine, then seal. Cook for 2 hours at 146 degrees F

Nutrition: calories 320, fat 23, fiber 0, carbs 12, protein 37

Garlic Chicken Bites

Preparation time: 10 minutes

Cooking time: 40 minutes

Servings: 6

Ingredients:
- ✓ 2 lb. chicken breast, skinless, boneless and cubed
- ✓ 4 garlic cloves, minced

- ✓ 2 tbsp. olive oil
- ✓ 1 tbsp. balsamic vinegar
- ✓ ½ cup honey
- ✓ A pinch of salt and black pepper
- ✓ ½ tsp. hot paprika

Directions:

1. After mixing the chicken with the garlic and other ingredients in a sealed sous vide bag, cook the mixture for 40 minutes in a water oven at 180 degrees Fahrenheit.
2. Place it on a dish to be ready as an appetiser.

Nutrition: calories 234, fat 11, fiber 3, carbs 20, protein 12

Chocolate Chili Cake

Servings: 6
Cooking Time: 1 Hour 15 Minutes

Ingredients:

- ✓ 4 Medium eggs
- ✓ 4ounces unsalted butter
- ✓ 2 tbsp. cocoa powder
- ✓ ½ pounds chocolate chips
- ✓ ½ tsp. chili powder
- ✓ ¼ cup brown sugar

Directions:

1. The recommended temperature for a sous vide cooker is 115 °F.Put the Sous Vide bag with the butter and chocolate chips inside. It should spend 15 minutes in a kettle of boiling water.

2. Get rid of the bag and lower the oven's temperature to 170 degrees.
3. Make a batch of 6 ounces right now. Mason jars with cooking spray Beat the eggs and brown sugar until they are fluffy and light.
4. Add the chocolate, chilli powder, and cocoa powder. To store, divide the mixture equally among clean mason jars and lightly screw on the lids. The jars should be placed in a water bath and left there for an hour. Long-lasting methods: To stop the cooking, remove the jars and place them on a cooling rack. Place the cake on a serving dish by turning it over.
5. Serve the dessert with raspberry ice cream.

Matcha Ice Cream

Servings: 1
Cooking Time: 1 Hour

Ingredients:

- ✓ 2 cups half-and-half
- ✓ 3 tbsp. matcha (green tea powder)
- ✓ ½ cup granulated sugar
- ✓ ⅛ tsp. kosher salt

Directions:

1. Bring the bath's water temperature up to 185 degrees. In a medium bowl, combine the half-and-half, matcha, sugar, and salt. With a fast pass of a hand flame or by carefully scooping them out with a spoon, foam or bubbles may be eliminated. Place the ingredients for the ice cream in a bag that can be sealed.
2. Make sure to seal it using the water displacement procedure and double it up. Start the timer and set the sous vide for one hour of cooking. In a medium basin, combine equal parts of ice and

cold water to make an ice bath. Place the bag in the ice bath to cool it after 15 to 20 minutes, and then chill it for an hour in the refrigerator.

3. Use a refrigerated bowl and the manufacturer's directions to create ice cream. The precise time required for churning will vary from machine to machine, but 15-20 minutes is a decent generalization.

4. The ice cream should be frozen for at least an hour, ideally longer, in an airtight container.

5. The ice cream can only be kept for a week at most.

Hot Spiced Cider

Preparation time: 5 minutes
Cooking time: 1 hour
Servings: 6

Ingredients

✓ 2 bottles apple cider

✓ 1 cinnamon stick

✓ 1 tbsp. maple syrup

✓ ½ tsp. black peppercorns

✓ 2 tbsp. orange juice

Directions:

1. To prepare a Sous Vide meal, place your immersion circulator in your water bath and warm it to roughly 140 degrees Fahrenheit. Place everything in a medium plastic bag with a closure.

2. We must submerge the thing before sealing it. The suggested cooking time is one hour. Strain the mixture before serving it chilled.

Nutrition: Calories 96, Carbohydrates 24 g, Fats 0 g, Protein 0 g

Spiced Coconut Ice Cream

Preparation Time: 60 minutes
Cooking Time: 30 minutes

Servings: 4

Ingredients

- ✓ 1 can (13 ounces) full-fat coconut milk
- ✓ ¾ cup sugar
- ✓ ½ tsp. kosher salt
- ✓ 2 tsp. vanilla extract
- ✓ ½ tsp. ground cinnamon
- ✓ ¼ tsp. nutmeg
- ✓ ¼ tsp. coriander
- ✓ 4 Medium egg yolks
- ✓ Tools required
- ✓ Ice Cream Maker

Directions:

1. A Sous Vide immersion circulator that is set to 180 degrees Fahrenheit should be used to prepare a water bath.
2. In a medium saucepan, combine the coconut milk, salt, sugar, cinnamon, vanilla, nutmeg, and coriander.
3. Bring to a boil. Remove the food from the heat when it has completed cooking and let it rest for 30 minutes. After adding the ingredients and egg yolks to the blender, mix for 30 seconds. The mixture should be poured into and sealed in a resealable plastic bag.
4. Shake the bag periodically throughout the 30 minutes of preparation.
5. Put the bag in an ice bath, then churn the ingredients in an ice cream machine.

6. Place it on the table once you've frozen it.

Nutrition: Calories: 693|Carbohydrate: 36g|Protein: 9g|Fat: 60g|Sugar: 32g|Sodium: 183mg

Cold Brew Coffee

Servings:x
Cooking Time:x

Ingredients:

- ✓ ¾ Cup Fresh, Coarsely Ground Coffee
- ✓ 4 Cups of Water
- ✓ Equipment
- ✓ 2 16oz Mason Jars

Directions:

1. Set the water bath to 150 °F. Make sure the coffee beans are coarsely ground if you're cold brewing.
2. In a medium bowl, combine the water and coffee grounds; stir until the coffee is thoroughly wet. Give each mason jar an equal amount of the coffee mixture, leaving a half-inch headroom at the top.
3. Tighten the lids of the Mason jars with your fingers to seal them. Because air must escape while heating, overtightening the lid runs the risk of shattering the glass. Set up a water bath and add the canning jars.
4. Plan on cooking the food for two hours. Coffee should be removed from its containers, filtered through cheesecloth or a coffee filter, and then placed in the refrigerator to chill. Pour over ice and serve.

Strawberry Basil Shrub

Servings: 12
Cooking Time: 120 Minutes

Ingredients:

- ✓ 1 pound's fresh strawberries, trimmed
- ✓ 1 pound's ultrafine sugar
- ✓ 2 cups balsamic vinegar
- ✓ 1 cup water
- ✓ 1 cup fresh basil leaves

Directions:

1. For Sous Vide cooking, preheat your immersion circulator to 135 degrees Fahrenheit and fill a medium saucepan with water. Place everything in a medium plastic bag with a closure. We must submerge the thing before sealing it.
2. It should cook for two hours in the oven. When the bag is done cooking, remove it from the water and drain the contents through a wire mesh strainer into a medium basin.
3. Place in the refrigerator, then enjoy cold!

Mango Pistachio Rice Pudding

Servings:4
Cooking Time:x

Ingredients:

- ✓ 11/3 cups whole milk
- ✓ 2/3 cup heavy cream
- ✓ 3 Medium eggs
- ✓ 1/2 cup granulated sugar
- ✓ 1 tsp. vanilla extract
- ✓ 2 cups cooked white rice (long grain or jasmine)
- ✓ 1/2 cup diced dried mango
- ✓ 1/2 cup roughly chopped pistachios

Directions:

1. Pour water into the bathtub to use it. Set your sous vide machine's temperature to 83°C (183°F) to prepare your meal.
2. In a larger bowl, whisk the milk, cream, eggs, sugar, and vanilla until well combined.
3. After cooking, the rice and dried mango should be combined. Put the rice mixture in a plastic bag that has been vacuum-sealed. Make sure the rice mixture is distributed evenly throughout the bag.
4. Using the sous vide technique, cook the rice in a water bath for 40 to 45 minutes.
5. Before serving, place in dishes and top with pistachios. It may be served cold or heated.

Lemon Curd

Preparation time: 8 hours 10 minutes
Cooking time: 45 minutes
Servings: 3

Ingredients

- ✓ 6 tbsp. unsalted butter, melted, cooled
- ✓ 4 lemon juice
- ✓ 6 Medium egg yolks at room temperature
- ✓ 1 cup granulated sugar

Directions:

1. Set your Sous Vide immersion circulator to 179 degrees Fahrenheit and have your water bath ready.
2. Lemon juice, sugar, and butter should be combined.
3. After adding the egg yolks, whip the mixture until the sugar is completely dissolved. Use the water immersion procedure to thoroughly seal the resealable bag containing the eggs. 45

minutes of cooking after submersion Shake the bag vigorously inside the ice bag.
4. For at least 12 hours, refrigerate the curd.
5. The curd must next be whisked after being poured into a basin.
6. Use and dispense as necessary.

Nutrition: Calories 184, Carbohydrates 15 g, Fats 12 g, Protein 4 g

Sous Vide Crème Brulee

Preparation time: 10 minutes
Cooking time: 1 hour
Servings: 4

Ingredients:

- ✓ ¼ cup sugar
- ✓ 1 pinch salt
- ✓ 1 cup heavy cream
- ✓ 3 Medium egg yolks
- ✓ Brown sugar, to sprinkle

Directions:

1. Set the Sous Vide temperature to 181°F. Blend everything together in a blender.
2. Process until the mixture has a consistent consistency. Put the bag's contents in the sous vide machine. Squeeze as much air out of the sidewalls as you can.
3. Using a clip, fasten the bag to the edge of your pot. Cook the bag for 60 minutes in a water bath. Take the bag out and give it a moderate shake after the first thirty minutes. Please take the cooking bag out of the appliance.
4. Pour the contents of the bag into four ramekins to serve. Brown sugar should be added to the egg custard.
5. Sugar can be torch-made into caramel. Serve.

Nutrition: Calories 196, Carbohydrates 13.8 g, Fats 14.5 g, Protein 2.6 g

Orange Cream Cocktail

Servings: x
Cooking Time: 1½ Hours

Ingredients:

- ✓ 1/4 cup sugar
- ✓ 1 3/4 cups Vodka
- ✓ Zest of 3 Medium oranges
- ✓ 1 vanilla bean, seeds from inside the pod

Directions:

1. Attach the immersion circulator after heating water in a Cambro or other similar container to 130 degrees Fahrenheit. Put everything in a clean mason jar and give it a good shake. The seal must be tight at all times.
2. The jar should be cooked in a water bath sous vide for around 1.5 hours.
3. Put it in a medium dish of cold water after you've removed it from the sous vide. Use a fine-mesh sieve to filter the contents.
4. Once the orange peel and vanilla bean fragments have been removed, the mixture may be kept in the refrigerator for up to a month in a sealed container.

Maple Raisin Rice Pudding

Preparation Time: 10 minutes
Cooking Time: 120 minutes
Servings: 4

Ingredients

- ✓ 3 cups skim milk
- ✓ 2 tbsp. butter
- ✓ 2 cups Arborio rice
- ✓ ½ cup maple syrup
- ✓ 2 tsp. ground cinnamon
- ✓ ½ tsp. ground ginger
- ✓ Ground cinnamon/cinnamon sugar for serving

Directions:

1. A 140°F water bath should be ready, and your Sous Vide immersion circulator should be turned on. Combine all of the ingredients—aside from the cinnamon—in a resealable bag. We must submerge the thing before sealing it.
2. 2 hours at 200 degrees in the oven. After the allotted time has passed, remove the ingredients from the water and combine them.
3. Put a scoop of the pudding on each serving plate. Sprinkle with cinnamon before serving while still hot.

Nutrition: Calories: 300| Carbohydrate: 49g|Protein: 6g|Fat: 8g |Sugar: 18gSodium: 140mg

Pineapple Rum

Preparation Time: 15 minutes
Cooking Time: 120 minutes

Servings: 12

Ingredients

- ✓ 1 peeled and cored pineapple cut into 1-inch pieces
- ✓ 1 bottle dark rum
- ✓ 1 cup granulated sugar

Directions:

1. For Sous Vide cooking, set up your immersion circulator and raise the water's temperature to 135 degrees Fahrenheit. Use the immersion method to close a resealable zipper bag with the pineapple, rum, and sugar inside.
2. Keep the meal immersed and cooking underwater for approximately two hours. Then, transfer the bowl's contents into a medium bowl after passing them through a metal mesh strainer.
3. After at least eight hours of chilling in the refrigerator, serve.

Nutrition: Calories: 442Carbohydrate: 45g|Protein: 1g|Fat: 0g|Sugar: 54g|Sodium: 8mg

The Ultimate Creme Brulee!

Servings:x
Cooking Time: 45 Minutes

Ingredients:

- ✓ 2 cup of heavy whipping cream
- ✓ 4 Medium egg yolks
- ✓ ¼ cup of granulated sugar
- ✓ Suggested Optional ingredients for variation
- ✓ ½ a tsp. of ground vanilla
- ✓ 1 tsp. of rose water
- ✓ 1 tsp. of orange blossom water
- ✓ Earl Grey tea bag
- ✓ 1 tbsp. of ginger
- ✓ 2 tbsp. of instant Espresso
- ✓ ¼ tsp. of flavor extract such as peppermint, almond, orange, anise etc.
- ✓ Fresh sprigs of basil, mint, rosemary or tarragon
- ✓ Tsp. of dried lavender

Directions:

1. Heat water in a medium saucepan to 115 degrees Fahrenheit before beginning to cook with a sous vide machine. In a medium bowl, combine the sugar and egg yolks and whisk until the mixture is light in color.
2. In a small pan over medium heat, bring heavy cream to a simmer. You can flavor the cream however you like while it's hot. The crème brulee with the greatest tradition uses a vanilla bean stick.
3. Three to four minutes on low heat is the suggested cooking time. Remove the heart from the pan and let it cool for about Start by pouring a little.
4. Use a whisk to completely combine. Then, combine the other ingredients from the bowl into the cream while briskly whisking them through the sieve. Equal quantities should be placed in each of the four jars. Be sure there is room between the lid and the jar when you screw it on to prevent the jars from bursting after they are immersed. In a water bath, place the bottles. Your water bath should simmer for 45 minutes with the cover on.
5. After removing the containers from the water, carefully dry them with a towel. After they have cooled, place them in the refrigerator and refrigerate for at least 4 hours. When you're ready to serve, remove them and pop the lid. Add half a teaspoon of sugar on top of your custards.
6. To get a caramelized finish, place it under a broiler or torch. Serve!

Irish Iced Coffee

Servings:x
Cooking Time: 6 Hours

Ingredients:
- ✓ For Coffee:

- ✓ 3 cups bourbon
- ✓ ½ Cup whole coffee beans
- ✓ 2 tbsp. brown sugar
- ✓ For Serving:
- ✓ Ice, as required
- ✓ 2 ounces infused whiskey
- ✓ 1 ounce heavy cream

Directions:

2. Use an adjustable clamp to secure a sous vide immersion circulator to the Cambro container or pot carrying the water after preheating it to 165 degrees Fahrenheit. Put all the ingredients in a bag and heat them.
3. The bag should be properly shut once the air has been taken out. After inserting the pouch into a water bath in a sous vide cooker, cook for about 6 hours. Shake the bag vigorously after removing it from the water bath.
4. Soak in a medium dish of cold water for at least 30 minutes. Through the sieve, transfer the bowl's contents to the holding container.
5. Individual serving glasses with ice and whiskey should be placed on the table for visitors. Pour the whiskey mixture into each of your glasses.
6. Serve after adding a dollop of whipped cream to the dish.

Strawberry Mousse

Servings: 4

Cooking Time: 45 Minutes

Ingredients:

- ✓ ½ pounds strawberries
- ✓ 1 ½ tbsp. lemon juice
- ✓ 3 tbsp. fine sugar

- ✓ ½ cup heavy cream
- ✓ ½ tsp. vanilla paste

Directions:

1. 180°F is the ideal cooking temperature. In a Sous vide bag, combine the strawberries, sugar, and lemon juice. To make sure the bag is closed, use the water immersion method.
2. Cook the bag for 45 minutes in a water bath. Long-lasting methods: Remove the bag from your sous vide cooker. Blend the berries in a blender until they are completely smooth. Process until the mixture has a consistent consistency. Until the mixture reaches room temperature, put the bowl in a cool location. Whip the heavy cream and vanilla until firm peaks form while you wait.
3. Mix in the strawberry purée after adding it. Four dishes should each contain some mousse. Before serving, make sure to chill for at least an hour.

Soft Cranberry Pears

Servings: 4

Cooking Timex

Ingredients:

- ✓ 2 ounces water
- ✓ 6 tbsp. cranberry jam
- ✓ ¼ cup sugar
- ✓ 1 tsp. salt
- ✓ 4 pears, rinsed, peeled, cored, halved

Directions:

1. Set the sous vide to 185 degrees Fahrenheit for preparation. Jam, sugar, salt, and a little water may be whisked together to create an easy sauce.
2. Place the pears in the mixture after coating them. Put the pears in a Medium ziplock bag or a vacuum-seal bag to keep them in the sauce for later.
3. To remove any leftover air, use a vacuum sealer or the water displacement method. Cook the pears for an hour, or until they are soft but still have some bite, in the sealed bag in the water bath.
4. Take it out of the pouch after you're done eating it, then serve it with a scoop of vanilla ice cream.

Warm Peach Cobbler

Servings: 6

Cooking Time:x

Ingredients:

- ✓ 1 cup self-rising flour
- ✓ 1 cup granulated sugar
- ✓ 1 cup whole milk
- ✓ 1 tsp. vanilla extract
- ✓ 1 stick unsalted butter, melted
- ✓ 2 cup roughly chopped peaches

Directions:

1. The temperature on your sous vide machine has to be 195 degrees Fahrenheit.
2. Spray six half-pint canning jars generously with nonstick oil or butter to prepare them. Use a whisk to blend the flour and sugar in a medium bowl. While continuously whisking, gradually add the milk and vanilla extract. Mix thoroughly before adding the peaches and melted butter.

3. Whisk the batter ingredients together in another bowl. To let any trapped air out, give each jar a solid tap on the counter. Be careful not to overtighten the lids of the jars, as this will allow steam to escape.
4. Seal the jars until they are snug. After placing the jars in the water bath, set the timer for three hours. Put the finished jars on a cooling rack and let them cool for at least 10 minutes before serving.
5. The ideal accompaniment would be a spoonful of vanilla ice cream.

Classic Chocolate Pudding

Servings: 5

Cooking Time: 1 Hour

Ingredients:

- ✓ ¼ cup cornstarch
- ✓ 8 tbsp. sugar, divided
- ✓ 2 tbsp. cocoa powder
- ✓ 2 cups whole milk
- ✓ ¾ cup light cream
- ✓ 2 Medium egg yolks
- ✓ ½ tsp. salt

Directions:

1. To 176°F, heat the water bath. With a fork, thoroughly mix the cornstarch and 6 tbsp.
2. sugar in a small bowl, breaking up any lumps. Whisk the cornstarch mixture with the sugar and cocoa powder in a medium saucepan over medium-low heat. Add the milk and cream gradually while mixing with a whisk. Stirring regularly with a rubber spatula can help you avoid being burned while heating the liquid until it comes to a boil.

3. The liquid will gradually begin to thicken. In a medium bowl, combine the egg yolks with the remaining 2 tablespoons of sugar and the salt.
4. Whisk the ingredients together. You must gently pour the hot milk mixture into the egg mixture if you don't want your eggs to curdle. It is advised to increase the pour rate gradually. Filter this mixture using a strainer with a fine mesh.
5. Five 8-ounce Mason jars should be filled and finger-sealed as securely as possible. Set the timer for one hour and gently place the containers in the hot sous vide water
6. With a pair of tongs, remove the pudding jars from the water and set them aside to cool for 15 to 30 minutes before serving. After overnight refrigeration, serve the contents of the jars.

Cranberry Vodka

Servings:x

Cooking Time: 2 Hours 15 Mins

Ingredients:

- ✓ For Vodka:
- ✓ 4 cups vodka
- ✓ ¾ Of a pound fresh cranberries
- ✓ For Simple Syrup:
- ✓ 2½ cups water
- ✓ 2 cups sugar

Directions:

1. Put water in the pot or Cambro, clamp the immersion circulator to it, and then heat it to 153 degrees Fahrenheit. In a cooking bag, combine the vodka and cranberries.
2. The bag should be properly shut once the air has been taken out. Set the timer for around two hours and place the pouch in the water bath.

3. Remove the bag from the water bath, then gently open it. Place the strained mixture in a bottle that has a secure cover.
4. To produce simple syrup, combine equal parts water and sugar in a pot and cook over medium-high heat. Stir it periodically for approximately 15 minutes while it simmers. Remove from the heat and let cool.
5. Once the vodka has cooled, combine it completely with the sugar syrup.

Coconut Milk Kheer

Servings:2

Cooking Time:3 Hours.

Ingredients:

- ✓ 30ml basmati rice
- ✓ 1 cup coconut milk whole.
- ✓ 1 cup water
- ✓ Granulated sugar.
- ✓ Cardamom pods.

Directions:

1. Place two rice containers in the refrigerator. After whisking the remaining ingredients, divide the mixture into the two jars.
2. After being placed in a water bath for two hours, serve with pudding on top..

Carrot Pudding

Servings: 4

Cooking Time:x

Ingredients:

- ✓ 1 cup sugar or to taste

- ✓ 1 tbsp. almonds
- ✓ ½ tsp. ground cardamom
- ✓ 1-pound carrots, grated
- ✓ 2 cups milk
- ✓ 1 tbsp. pistachios
- ✓ 1 tbsp. raisins
- ✓ 1 tbsp. ghee
- ✓ Extra nuts and raisins for garnishing

Directions:

1. Set the sous vide to 185 degrees Fahrenheit for preparation. Soak the nuts in water for at least 30 minutes, or until the raisins are full. Combine the carrots, raisins, pistachios, almonds, and other ingredients in a medium ziplock bag or a vacuum-sealed bag.
2. To remove any leftover air, use a vacuum sealer or the water displacement method.
3. After closing the bag, cook it in a water bath for two hours. Put a pot on low heat in the meantime. Add milk and simmer for one hour. Add sugar and stir until all of the sugar has been dissolved.
4. After the allotted time has passed, remove the carrots from their bag and water and put them in a saucepan with the milk. For five minutes, set the timer.
5. Add some cardamom powder, stir often, and continue to simmer.
6. As a garnish, you may add more nuts and raisins. Prepare your food either hot or cold.

Limoncello Vodka Cocktail

Servings: 5

Cooking Time: 180 Minutes

Ingredients:

- ✓ 1 bottle vodka
- ✓ Grated zest/peel of 10-15 thoroughly washed lemons
- ✓ 1 cup granulated sugar
- ✓ 1 cup water

Directions:

1. For Sous Vide cooking, preheat your immersion circulator to 135 degrees Fahrenheit and fill a medium saucepan with water. The vodka and lemon zest should be placed in a medium zip-top bag and immersion-sealed.
2. Spend two to three hours gently cooking food. With a pot, have a medium flame ready. Combine the sugar and water to produce the syrup, then mix until the sugar is dissolved.
3. After soaking, take out the bag and empty the contents into a dish using a metal mesh strainer.
4. Add the syrup and stir. Serve after adding limoncello to the bottles!

Pears With Port

Servings:4

Cooking Time:x

Ingredients:

- ✓ 2 cups port
- ✓ 1/4 cup granulated sugar
- ✓ 1 cinnamon stick
- ✓ 1 whole star anise
- ✓ 2 whole cloves
- ✓ 4 pears (Anjou, Bartlett, or other), peeled, halved, and cored

Directions:

1. In a small saucepan, warm the port, sugar, cinnamon stick, star anise, and cloves.
2. Once the mixture begins to boil, lower the heat and whisk regularly.
3. At least two minutes are required for the sauce to simmer. Turn off the heat and throw the cloves, star anise, and cinnamon stick into the pan.
4. Allow the sauce to reheat to room temperature while you unwind. Pour water into the bathtub to use it. Set your sous vide machine's temperature to 83°C (183°F) to prepare your meal.
5. For storage, combine the sauce with the pear halves in a vacuum-sealed bag. Instead of piling the pears, arrange them in a single, flat layer. Using the sous vide technique, cook the pears in a water bath for 45 minutes.
6. Take the pears out of the water and immediately submerge them in the ice bath to stop them from cooking any more. After cutting the bag open, the sauce may be put into a pot. Over medium heat, let the sauce thicken and decrease.
7. Divide the reduced syrup between the two pear halves and place one on a plate to serve.

Infused Olive Oil

Servings:x

Cooking Time:x

Ingredients:

- ✓ 2 cups
- ✓ Dried Infusion Flavorings of choice, or try one of these:
- ✓ For Chili Herb Oil
- ✓ 2 tbsp.
- ✓ For Vanilla Olive Oil
- ✓ 2 vanilla bean pods, split and seeded; use both pods and seeds to infuse

✓ Note: Special care should be taken to use only clean dried herbs and flavorings when infusing oils because of the risk of soil contamination.

Directions:

1. The bath's water needs to be heated to 73 degrees. A plastic bag that can be sealed should be used to store olive oil. Add the selected seasonings.
2. It is advised to first remove the air using the displacement method before sealing the joint. In a water bath, cook the pouch for three hours.
3. When you're done with the water bath, place the pouch in an ice bath. You may need to filter the oil before putting it in the refrigerator, depending on the substances used in the infusion.
4. The oil may either be moved to a glass container with a screw-top lid or maintained permanently in the bag.
5. Refrigerator storage time: two to four months.

Egg With Avocado, Spinach And Parmesan On A Muffin

Servings:x

Cooking Time:x

Ingredients:

✓ 1 egg
✓ Half a muffin
✓ A few spinaches leave
✓ Quarter of an avocado, sliced
✓ Few grates of Parmesan
✓ Salt and pepper to taste

Directions:

1. Reach 167 degrees Fahrenheit using the water bath. Make sure to properly place the egg in the water bath. You can cook it in about 13 minutes.
2. Place the broiler under the muffin half. Place several slices of avocado on the bagel. Add spinach leaves and avocado to a plate. Once the egg is cooked to the appropriate doneness, it is time to remove it from the water.
3. Serve the spinach with the egg gently cracked over it. Add some Parmesan cheese that has been granted.
4. Season with salt and pepper to taste just before serving.

Lemon Turmeric Energy Bites

Makes 30 balls | **Prep. time** 10 minutes

Ingredients

- ✓ 2 cups raw nuts: cashews, walnuts, pecans, or your choice
- ✓ 1 cup desiccated coconut
- ✓ ¼ cup coconut butter (NOT coconut oil)
- ✓ ¾ teaspoon turmeric
- ✓ ¼ cup lemon juice
- ✓ 1 tablespoon lemon zest
- ✓ 2 scoops collagen peptides (or protein powder. Omit if desired.)
- ✓ Pinch sea salt and black pepper

(Optional) Toppings

- ✓ Shredded coconut and lemon zest (about 1 teaspoon lemon zest and ¼ cup shredded coconut)

Directions

1. The nuts should be processed in a food processor in batches until they resemble flour.
2. Then process until a dough forms in the food processor with the other ingredients.

3. The dough should be formed into balls, which should then be covered with coconut or lemon zest. If desired, roll the balls on a paper towel to absorb any leftover oil.
4. These little balls may be stored in the refrigerator in an airtight jar for 3 to 4 weeks.

Nutrition (per serving): Calories 78, fat 6 g, carbs 3 g, protein 2 g, sodium 9 mg

Lemon Turmeric Energy Bites

Makes 30 balls | **Prep. time** 10 minutes

Ingredients

- ✓ 2 cups raw nuts: cashews, walnuts, pecans, or your choice
- ✓ 1 cup desiccated coconut
- ✓ ¼ cup coconut butter (NOT coconut oil)
- ✓ ¾ teaspoon turmeric
- ✓ ¼ cup lemon juice
- ✓ 1 tablespoon lemon zest
- ✓ 2 scoops collagen peptides (or protein powder. Omit if desired.)
- ✓ Pinch sea salt and black pepper

(Optional) Toppings

- ✓ Shredded coconut and lemon zest (about 1 teaspoon lemon zest and ¼ cup shredded coconut)

Directions

1. The nuts should be processed in a food processor in batches until they resemble flour.
2. Then process until a dough form in the food processor with the other ingredients.

3. The dough should be formed into balls, which should then be covered with coconut or lemon zest. If desired, roll the balls on a paper towel to absorb any leftover oil.
4. These little balls may be stored in the refrigerator in an airtight jar for 3 to 4 weeks.

Nutrition (per serving): Calories 78, fat 6 g, carbs 3 g, protein 2 g, sodium 9 mg

Spicy Pumpkin Hummus

Serves 7 | Prep. time 10 minutes

Ingredients

- ✓ 1 (15 ounce) can chickpeas, rinsed and drained
- ✓ ½ cup canned pumpkin
- ✓ 2 tablespoons extra-virgin olive oil
- ✓ 2 tablespoons fresh lemon juice
- ✓ 1 small clove garlic
- ✓ 1 teaspoon ground smoked paprika
- ✓ ¾ teaspoon ground cumin
- ✓ ½ teaspoon chili powder
- ✓ ½ teaspoon ground turmeric
- ✓ ½ teaspoon sea salt or to taste.

Directions

1. Pulse all the ingredients in a blender or food processor until they are well combined.
2. Add any desired garnishes after transferring the hummus to a serving dish. accompanied by veggies.

Nutrition (per serving) Calories 98, fat 5 g, carbs 10 g, protein 3 g, sodium 336 mg

Anti-Inflammatory Juice

Serves 2 | Prep. time 5 minutes

Ingredients

- ✓ 2 cups pineapple pieces (frozen is best)
- ✓ 1 cup cucumber, peeled and chopped
- ✓ 1 tablespoon lime juice
- ✓ 1 jalapeño, deseeded and chopped
- ✓ 1 tablespoon fresh mint leaves (packed) plus more for garnish

Directions

1. If you have a juicer, this recipe works best for you; otherwise, you may use a food processor or blender.
2. Serve over ice after combining all the ingredients in a blender.

Nutrition (per serving) Calories 94, fat 0 g, carbs 23 g, protein 1 g, sodium 3 mg

Coconut and Sweet Potato Muffins

Makes 12 muffins | **Prep. time** 20 minutes |

Cooking time 35 minutes

Ingredients

- ✓ 1 small sweet potato, roasted (1 cup, packed)
- ✓ ¾ cup coconut milk
- ✓ ½ cup maple syrup
- ✓ 3 eggs, lightly beaten
- ✓ 2 tablespoons olive oil
- ✓ 1 cup brown rice flour
- ✓ ¼ cup coconut flour
- ✓ 1 tablespoon ground cinnamon
- ✓ ½ teaspoon salt
- ✓ ⅛ teaspoon ground cloves
- ✓ 1 teaspoon ground ginger
- ✓ 1 tablespoon baking powder
- ✓ ⅛ teaspoon ground nutmeg

Directions

1. Set the oven to 400°F. You may either line a muffin pan with liners or use nonstick cooking spray.
2. In a mixing dish, combine the cooked sweet potato with the coconut milk and maple syrup, and stir to combine. Mix thoroughly after adding the eggs and oil. Combine the flours, salt, cinnamon, cloves, ginger, baking powder, and nutmeg in a separate mixing dish.
3. Mix the spices well, then gradually incorporate the mixture into the sweet potato mixture.
4. Place the pan on the middle oven rack after filling the muffin cups about two-thirds of the way.
5. 30 minutes is the estimated baking time. To check whether they are cooked through, use a toothpick.

Nutrition (per serving) Calories 147, fat 4 g, carbs 24 g, protein 3 g, sodium 145 mg

Ginger Turmeric Shots

Serves 4 | **Prep. time** 10 minutes

Ingredients

- ✓ 4 inches turmeric (1 teaspoon of powder equals 1 inch of root)
- ✓ 4 inches fresh ginger
- ✓ 2 oranges
- ✓ 4 cloves garlic

Directions

1. All ingredients should be put through the juicer (or food processor) individually before being combined in a pitcher.
2. Pour into shot glasses after thoroughly mixing. Drink right away.

Nutrition (per serving) Calories 50, fat 3 g, carbs 12 g, protein 1 g, sodium 4 mg

Chocolate Chia Seed Pudding

Chia seeds and chocolate are both high in antioxidants. Add the benefits of turmeric, and you have either a healthy breakfast or a flavorful dessert!

Serves 2 | **Prep. time** 3 minutes | **refrigeration time** 4 hours

Ingredients

- ✓ 1 can coconut milk (full fat)
- ✓ ⅓ cup chia seeds
- ✓ ¼ cup unsweetened cocoa powder
- ✓ 1 teaspoon ground turmeric
- ✓ ½ teaspoon cinnamon
- ✓ 1 teaspoon vanilla extract
- ✓ Pinch salt
- ✓ 2 tablespoons maple syrup
- ✓ Toppings: berries or nuts

Directions

1. Blend all the ingredients well in a high-powered blender or food processor
2. For at least 4 hours, or until thick, cover and chill. The finest is overnight.
3. Divide into individual servings and top with your preferred garnish.

Nutrition (per serving) Calories 284, fat 17 g, carbs 36 g, protein 10 g, sodium 82 mg

Chai Spice and Pear Oatmeal

This delicious and warming oatmeal is a healthy way to start your day.

Serves 4 | **Prep. time** 5 minutes | **Cooking time** 10 minutes

Ingredients

- ✓ 2 cups cooked spaghetti squash
- ✓ 2 medium pears, peeled, cored, and chopped (about 1 ½ cups)
- ✓ ½ cup apple cider or apple juice
- ✓ ¼ cup coconut milk
- ✓ 1 teaspoon cinnamon
- ✓ ¼ teaspoon ginger
- ✓ ⅛ teaspoon cloves
- ✓ ⅛ teaspoon nutmeg
- ✓ Pinch salt

Directions

1. All the ingredients should be combined in a small pot before being heated to a simmer. Cook it for 6 minutes, or until it thickens.
2. To get an oatmeal-like texture, use an immersion blender.
3. Serve with any extra toppings you choose.

Nutrition (per serving) Calories 218, fat 1 g, carbs 54 g, protein 1 g, sodium 130 mg

Mediterranean Quinoa Bowls

Serves 6 | **Prep. time** 15 minutes

Ingredients

- ✓ Roasted Red Pepper Sauce:
- ✓ 1 (16 ounce) jar roasted red peppers, drained (or roast your own)
- ✓ 1 clove garlic
- ✓ ½ teaspoon salt (more to taste)
- ✓ Juice of one lemon
- ✓ ¼ cup olive oil
- ✓ ½ cup almonds

For the bowls:

- ✓ 3 cups cooked quinoa
- ✓ 3 cups spinach or kale
- ✓ 1 cup chopped cucumber
- ✓ ½ cup feta cheese
- ✓ ½ cup kalamata olives
- ✓ 1 cup red onion, thinly sliced

Options:

- ✓ hummus
- ✓ fresh basil or parsley
- ✓ olive oil, lemon juice, salt, pepper

Directions

1. Get the sauce ready. The sauce components should be combined in a food processor and pulsed until almost smooth. It must be substantial.
2. Create the bowls. Take some of the cooked quinoa first. After the red pepper sauce, scatter some of the other ingredients on top.

Nutrition (per serving) Calories 407, fat 23 g, carbs 41 g, protein 11 g, sodium 853 mg

Anti-Inflammatory Buddha Bowl

Serves 4 | **Prep. time** 10 minutes |

Cooking time 30 minutes

Ingredients

- ✓ 2 pounds cauliflower florets, stems removed
- ✓ 1 tablespoon plus one teaspoon extra-virgin olive oil, divided
- ✓ 1 teaspoon turmeric
- ✓ Salt and pepper
- ✓ 10 ounces kale, chopped

- ✓ 1 clove garlic, minced
- ✓ 8 medium beets, cooked, peeled, and chopped
- ✓ 2 avocados, cubed
- ✓ 2 cups fresh blueberries
- ✓ ⅓ cup raw walnuts, chopped

Directions

1. Set the oven to 425 °F. Spray coconut or olive oil on the foil that you use to line a baking sheet. Combine 1 tablespoon of the olive oil and the turmeric with the sliced cauliflower.
2. Set it up on the prepared baking sheet.
3. Add salt and pepper, then place the tray in the oven. For around 30 minutes, bake. One teaspoon of olive oil should be heated in a large pan when the cauliflower is nearly done. When the kale begins to wilt after being added, add the garlic.
4. Put the bowls together after the greens and cauliflower are finished.
5. Kale should be the base, followed by walnuts, avocado, blueberries, cauliflower, and beets. Enjoy after serving!

Nutrition (per serving) Calories 450, fat 27 g, carbs 49 g, protein 13 g, sodium 377 mg

Chai Spice and Pear Oatmeal

This delicious and warming oatmeal is a healthy way to start your day.

Serves 4 | **Prep. time** 5 minutes |

Cooking time 10 minutes

Ingredients

- ✓ 2 cups cooked spaghetti squash
- ✓ 2 medium pears, peeled, cored, and chopped (about 1 ½ cups)
- ✓ ½ cup apple cider or apple juice

- ✓ ¼ cup coconut milk
- ✓ 1 teaspoon cinnamon
- ✓ ¼ teaspoon ginger
- ✓ ⅛ teaspoon cloves
- ✓ ⅛ teaspoon nutmeg
- ✓ Pinch salt

Directions

1. All the ingredients should be combined in a small pot before being heated to a simmer.
2. Cook it for 6 minutes, or until it thickens. To get an oatmeal-like texture, use an immersion blender.
3. Serve with any extra toppings you choose.

Nutrition (per serving) Calories 218, fat 1 g, carbs 54 g, protein 1 g, sodium 130 mg

Honey Ginger Shrimp Bowls

Serves 2 | **Prep. time** 20 minutes |

Cooking time 6 minutes

Ingredients

For the shrimp:

- ✓ 2 tablespoons honey
- ✓ 2 tablespoons coconut aminos or soy sauce
- ✓ 1 teaspoon fresh ginger, minced
- ✓ 2 cloves garlic, minced
- ✓ 12 ounces large uncooked shrimp, peeled and deveined
- ✓ 2 teaspoons avocado oil
- ✓ Lime, sea salt, and freshly ground pepper to taste

For the salad:

- ✓ 4 cups greens of your choice

- ✓ ½ cup shredded carrots
- ✓ ½ cup shredded radishes
- ✓ 4 green onions, sliced
- ✓ ¼ cup cilantro, chopped
- ✓ 1 avocado, sliced

For the dressing:

- ✓ 2 tablespoons lime juice
- ✓ 2 tablespoons extra-virgin olive oil
- ✓ 2 teaspoons coconut aminos
- ✓ 1 tablespoon honey
- ✓ 1 clove garlic, minced
- ✓ ½ teaspoon ginger powder
- ✓ Sea salt and pepper to taste

Directions

1. As indicated under the shrimp ingredients, combine the honey, coconut aminos (or soy sauce), ginger, and garlic in a mixing bowl.
2. Pour the marinade mixture over the shrimp and close the bag. Make sure all of the shrimp are covered by manipulating the bag.
3. While you are making the salad and dressing, refrigerate. Heat the avocado oil in a large pan over medium-high heat. When it's heated, add the marinated shrimp and cook for approximately three minutes.
4. When the shrimp are completely cooked and the sauce has slightly thickened, turn the shrimp over and simmer for an additional three minutes. Add salt, pepper, and lime juice for seasoning.
5. In a large bowl, combine all the ingredients for the salad. The salad should be divided into two halves, with half the shrimp added to each.
6. Whisk all the ingredients together to make the dressing. Serve the salad with the dressing on top.

Nutrition (per serving) Calories 516, fat 32 g, carbs 47 g, protein 12 g, sodium 636 mg

Chicken and Cabbage Skillet

Serves 4 | **Prep. time** 5 minutes |

Cooking time 20 minutes

Ingredients

- ✓ 1 ½ pounds chicken breast or thighs, cubed
- ✓ 1 tablespoon avocado oil
- ✓ ½ head cabbage, chopped
- ✓ 1 tablespoon turmeric
- ✓ 1 teaspoon garlic powder
- ✓ ½ teaspoon sea salt
- ✓ 3 carrots, peeled and grated
- ✓ 6 green onions, chopped
- ✓ 3 cups spinach or kale
- ✓ 2 cups brown rice, cooked, for serving
- ✓ ½ cup fresh cilantro, chopped

Directions

1. In a skillet set over medium-high heat, warm the oil. The chicken pieces should be cooked in hot oil until browned on both sides.
2. Once the cabbage is cooked, add the salt, turmeric, and garlic powder and toss to combine.
3. Stir once more before adding the spinach, green onions, and carrots.
4. After 3 more minutes of cooking, turn off the heat and remove the skillet. Serve with cilantro on top and over brown rice.

Nutrition (per serving) Calories 422, fat 10 g, carbs 39 g, protein 45 g, sodium 460 mg

Curried Shrimp and Vegetables

Serves 4 | **Prep. time** 10 minutes

Cooking time 15 minutes

Ingredients

- ✓ 3 tablespoons coconut oil
- ✓ 1 onion, sliced
- ✓ 2 cups cauliflower, cut into florets
- ✓ 1 cup coconut milk
- ✓ 1 tablespoon curry powder
- ✓ ¼ cup fresh parsley, chopped
- ✓ 1 pound shrimp, tails removed

Directions

1. Melt the coconut oil over medium-high heat in a large skillet. Cook the cauliflower and onion together until they are tender. Curry, parsley, and coconut milk are added to the skillet.
2. You are free to add any other spices you choose. (You'll get even more anti-inflammatory benefits from turmeric.) 2 to 3 more minutes of cooking When the shrimp are opaque, stir them into the skillet.

Nutrition (per serving) Calories 332, fat 22 g, carbs 11 g, protein 24 g, sodium 309 mg

Detox Dried Fruit with Chestnut Honey

Total time: 10 mins| **Prep Time** 10 mins | **Cooking time:** | **Difficulty:** Easy

Serving size: 3

Ingredients:

- ✓ 1/2 cup of shelled walnuts
- ✓ 1/2 cup of cashews
- ✓ 1 cup of shelled almonds
- ✓ 1/4 cup of peanuts

✓ 3 tablespoons of chestnut honey, liquid, and brown
✓ 1/2 cup of blackberries

Directions:

1. Blend all of the dry fruit together in a blender for 20 seconds or so.
2. The washed blackberries and honey should be added to each of the three big glasses that have the chopped fruit in them. winter evenings

Nutritional Values: Calories: 95 kcal | Carbohydrates 2g| Protein 28g| Fat 30g| Fiber 35g

Chia Breadstick and cracker

Total time: 10 mins |**Prep Time** 10 mins |
Cooking time: | **Difficulty**: Easy
Serving size: 3

Ingredients:

✓ 2 cups of flour
✓ 1 cup of water
✓ 4 tablespoons of oil
✓ 2 ounces of chia seeds
✓ salt
✓ 1 teaspoon of yeast

To garnish

✓ Semolina
✓ Coarse salt
✓ oil to brush over the crackers

Directions:

1. In a bowl, combine the flour, water, chia seeds, oil, and salt. Make a nice, supple dough.

2. Try to make a square and thin form by spreading it out on a piece of parchment paper. Knife-cut the dough, re-knead the leftovers, and repeat the process.
3. To prevent the dough from expanding while cooking, prick it with a fork.
4. Add salt and a thin layer of oil to the surface. For around 20 minutes, bake at 395 °F in a preheated oven.
5. In an airless bag, serve or store.

Nutritional Values: Calories: 88 kcal |Carbohydrates 32g |Protein 11g | Fat 2g | Fiber 18g

Orange and Pumpkin Salad

Total time: 25 mins| **Prep Time** 10 mins |
Cooking time: 15 mins| **Difficulty:** Easy
Serving size: 5

Ingredients:

- ✓ 1/2 pumpkin, seedless, peeled, and cut into cubes
- ✓ 2 oranges, cut into wedges and then into 3 parts
- ✓ 1 teaspoon of not too spicy red pepper (optional)
- ✓ 1 ounce of oil
- ✓ salt and black pepper

Directions:

1. With a sprinkle of water and a cover, boil the pumpkin in a saucepan for 15 minutes.
2. When done, combine it with the oranges in a dish. Add the chili, if desired, and season with oil, salt, and pepper. Present fresh.

Nutritional Values: Calories: 72 kcal | Carbohydrates 38g |Protein 9g |Fat 1g | Fiber 29g

Biscuits bars

Total time: 25 mins |**Prep Time** 10 mins |
Cooking time: | **Difficulty:** Easy
Serving size: 10

Ingredients:

- ✓ 1/3 cup of butter
- ✓ 1 cup of sugar
- ✓ 2 large eggs
- ✓ 1 and 1/2 cup of flour
- ✓ yeast
- ✓ 1 ounce of milk

Directions:

1. Bake at 375 degrees Fahrenheit and cover a baking sheet with parchment paper.
2. Whip the butter and sugar using a kitchen whisk. Add the eggs next, and then the baking powder-containing flour. Stir continuously before adding the milk.
3. Place it in the pan and bake it for approximately 30 minutes, or until a toothpick inserted neatly emerges from the dough.
4. After cooling, serve.

Nutritional Values: Calories: 120 kcal |Carbohydrates 38g |Protein 27g | Fat 3g | Fiber 2g

Coconut Biscuits

Total time: 50 mins | **Prep Time** 10 mins|
Cooking time: 40 mins| **Difficulty:** Easy
Serving size: 6

Ingredients:

- ✓ 1 cup of flour
- ✓ 1 cup of sugar
- ✓ 1/2 cup of coconut flour

- ✓ 1 ounce of grated coconut
- ✓ 2 eggs
- ✓ 1 cup of coconut milk
- ✓ 1/2 cup of seed oil
- ✓ salt
- ✓ 1 pinch of yeast

Directions:

1. Make the cookie dough in a large bowl by combining the flour and coconut flour, then adding the sugar and shredded coconut and beginning to knead in the coconut milk.
2. When the dough starts to become too thick, add the sesame oil and salt.
3. Add the yeast last. In a lined pan, bake at 365 °F for 40 minutes. Let it cool after cooking before serving.

Nutritional Values: Calories: 134 kcal| Carbohydrates 26g |Protein 12g | Fat 19g | Fiber 4g

Garlic soup

Total time: 75 mins| **Prep Time** 10 mins
Cooking time: 60 mins| **Difficulty:** Easy
Serving size: 12

Ingredients:

- ✓ 10 cloves of garlic, crushed
- ✓ 3 potatoes, peeled
- ✓ 1 tablespoon of processed flour
- ✓ 2 large carrots
- ✓ 1 ounce of butter
- ✓ 1 teaspoon of the vegetable cube
- ✓ salt
- ✓ 1 teaspoon of garlic powder
- ✓ 1 tablespoon of Italian dressing

✓ 1 teaspoon of hot pepper (optional)

Directions:

1. Make a quick sauté with butter and garlic in a pan. Fill the pan 3/4 full and add the finely diced potatoes and flour as soon as the garlic turns brown.
2. Bring to a boil, and then simmer while covered. The carrots and cube should then be added. Add the other ingredients and, if desired, the chili after 40 minutes of simmering.
3. Serve after adding salt to taste. Remove the garlic cloves if you'd like, then sip the hot soup.
4. It may also be kept for six days in the refrigerator in an airtight container.

Nutritional Values: Calories: 89 kcal |Carbohydrates 18g |protein 8g | Fat 6g | Fiber 19g

Onion Soup

Total time: 70 mins| **Prep Time** 10 mins
| **Cooking time:** 60 mins | **Difficulty:** Easy
Serving size: 8

Ingredients:

✓ 4 large onions, peeled and cut into 4 parts
✓ 1 tablespoon of curry
✓ 1 tablespoon of the vegetable cube
✓ 1 tablespoon of processed flour
✓ 4 medium potatoes, peeled
✓ 2 carrots
✓ salt
✓ 1 teaspoon of onion powder
✓ 1 tablespoon of Italian dressing
✓ 1 drizzle of oil

Directions:

1. Make a quick sauté with the onions and oil in a skillet. Add water and bring to a boil after the onions start to turn brown.
2. Reduce the heat after it begins to boil before adding the flour and very finely diced potatoes. Add the cube and the carrots. For 40 minutes, cook.
3. Curry, onion powder, and Italian dressing should all be added. Cook for another 20 minutes, then serve hot.
4. In a closed container, you may also refrigerate for up to 5 days.

Nutritional Values: Calories: 94 kcal |Carbohydrates 19g | Protein 12g| Fat 4g | Fiber 22g

Pepper Soup

Total time: 75 mins | **Prep Time** 15 mins
| **Cooking time:** 60 mins |**Difficulty:** Easy
Serving size: 6

Ingredients:

- ✓ 2 yellow peppers
- ✓ 1 green pepper
- ✓ 1 red pepper
- ✓ 2 ounces of butter
- ✓ 1 large onion, peeled and finely chopped
- ✓ 1 teaspoon of garlic powder
- ✓ 1 tablespoon of Italian dressing
- ✓ 1 tablespoon of processed flour
- ✓ salt

Directions:

1. Remove the green stem from each pepper and, if desired, remove the interior seeds before chopping them all finely. In a large pot, combine the onion and butter and quickly sauté.
2. Add the water and bring it to a boil after the onion starts to turn brown.
3. Add the flour and peppers. Cook for at least 40 minutes with the lid on.
4. When the peppers are almost done cooking, add the Italian dressing and garlic powder and simmer for a further 20 minutes or so.
5. Serve warm.

Nutritional Values: Calories: 102 kcal| Carbohydrates 18g| Protein 16g | Fat 9g | Fiber 32g

Green Soup

Total time: 70 mins |**Prep Time** 20 mins

| **Cooking time:** 50 mins | **Difficulty:** Easy

Serving size: 10

Ingredients:

- ✓ 2 green peppers
- ✓ 1 stalk of celery
- ✓ 2 bay leaves
- ✓ 1 onion
- ✓ 2 potatoes, finely chopped and peeled
- ✓ 1 teaspoon of the vegetable cube
- ✓ salt

Directions:

1. Bring to a boil the celery, bay leaves, water, and salt in a big saucepan.
2. Cut the pepper into thin strips and add them to the pool while the water is heating.

3. When it boils, add the potatoes, stock cube, and finely chopped onion.
4. After approximately 50 minutes of cooking, pause, then serve.

Nutritional Values: Calories: 78 kcal| Carbohydrates 12g | Protein 14g | Fat 2g | Fiber 36g

cheeses Soup

Total time: 70 mins | **Prep Time** 10 mins
| **Cooking time:** 60 mins | **Difficulty:** Easy
Serving size: 5

Ingredients:

- ✓ 1 ounce of soft cheese cubes
- ✓ 1 ounce of shredded hard cheese
- ✓ 2 ounces of aged Parmesan, grated
- ✓ 3 ounces of drained mozzarella
- ✓ 2 potatoes, peeled
- ✓ 1 tablespoon of flour
- ✓ salt and black pepper for seasoning
- ✓ 1 teaspoon of chives

Directions:

1. Mix the first three types of cheese in a large bowl to prepare them.
2. They and the chives will taste better with a dash of black pepper. In a saucepan with flour and water, cook the potatoes that have been finely diced.
3. Boil for a moment, then turn down the heat. For 30 minutes, cook. After adding the cheeses, simmer for another hour, omitting the mozzarella. When finished, add the mozzarella and serve warm.
4. The cheese will ultimately melt in this manner and get stringy. Serve warm.

Nutritional Values: Calories: 98 kcal |Carbohydrates 19g | Protein 24g | Fat 19g | Fiber 3g

Boiled Vegetables Soup

Total time: 45 mins| **Prep Time** 5 mins
| **Cooking time:** 40 mins | **Difficulty:** Easy
Serving size: 9

Ingredients:

- ✓ 1 bunch of green lettuce
- ✓ 1 red pepper, thinly sliced and seedless
- ✓ 1 yellow pepper, thinly sliced and seedless
- ✓ 1 bay leaf
- ✓ 1 stalk of celery
- ✓ 2 potatoes, peeled and finely chopped
- ✓ 1 onion, peeled and finely chopped
- ✓ 1 bunch of curly lettuce
- ✓ salt
- ✓ 1 tablespoon of Italian dressing

Directions:

1. The peppers, salt, and water should be placed in a big pot and brought to a boil.
2. Cook with the cover on for approximately 20 minutes over low heat. Then combine the curly lettuce with the green lettuce, celery, potatoes, and onion.
3. Add the bay leaf after cooking for another 10 minutes. Salt and Italian seasoning are used to season.
4. Serve warm or store in the fridge for up to 8 days.

Nutritional Values: Calories: 70 kcal | Carbohydrates 15g | Protein 17g | Fat 1g| Fiber 28g

Spinach Soup

Total time: 40 mins | **Prep Time** 10 mins
| **Cooking time:** 30 mins | **Difficulty:** Easy
Serving size: 8

Ingredients:

- ✓ 3 pounds of fresh spinach
- ✓ 3 cloves of garlic
- ✓ 3 ounces of butter
- ✓ 1/2 onion, finely chopped and peeled
- ✓ 2 potatoes, peeled
- ✓ 1 tablespoon of Italian dressing
- ✓ salt

Directions:

1. Quickly sauté the butter and garlic in a pot. Combine with the onion.
2. Cook on high heat for a little while. Add the water, potatoes, and spinach after the garlic and onion have started to brown. With the cover on and a low burner, bring to a boil and simmer for around 30 minutes.
3. Turn off the heat when the soup reaches the proper consistency and serve it hot with freshly grated cheese

Nutritional Values: Calories: 85 kcal | Carbohydrates 12g | Protein 20g | Fat 12g | Fiber 19g

Super Burger with Bacon and Onions

Servings: 8

Nutrition: 876 Calories,

53g Fat, 26g Carbohydrates, 69g Protein

Ingredients:

- ✓ 8 slices onions
- ✓ 16 slices thin bacon
- ✓ salt and pepper
- ✓ 8 slices cheese
- ✓ 8 hamburger buns
- ✓ 3 pounds ground beef
- ✓ 8 slices thick-cut bacon

Directions:

1. Slice your onion into 3/4-inch-thick pieces. Make 8 balls of the same size from the hamburgers. Sprinkle salt and pepper generously over the top.
2. Warm up your griddle by turning the heat up to high or medium. With a sturdy spatula, place the burger balls on the grill and thoroughly press them down. Cook the burger on the grill for a few minutes, or until a deep-brown crust develops, before seasoning the raw side and flipping.
3. Grill for a few more minutes, or until the bottom has developed a crust as well, while covering with a melting lid.
4. Serve right away after taking the food from the griddle!

Crunchy and super tasty Hash Browns

Servings: 6

Nutrition: 774 Calories,

60g Fat, 36g Carbohydrates, 25g Protein

Ingredients:

- ✓ 1/4 cup finely diced onions (optional)
- ✓ 1/4 cup butter
- ✓ 1/2-pound breakfast sausage links, sliced
- ✓ 6 eggs, whisked
- ✓ 1/4 cup whole milk
- ✓ 1/4 - 1/3 cup oil

- ✓ 3 cups dehydrated hash browns
- ✓ 3 cups hot water
- ✓ Salt, pepper, and garlic
- ✓ 2 cups shredded cheddar cheese

Directions:

1. Hash browns and boiling water should be combined in a basket and submerged for approximately 15 minutes. Eliminate any extra water.
2. As the hash browns cook, warm your gas griddle over medium-low heat. With roughly a tablespoon of butter, grill the onions for three to four minutes. Place the hash browns on the griddle and top with one or two tablespoons of oil.
3. Cook the chopped sausages and scramble the eggs in the remaining butter while the hashbrowns are cooking. You two can work on this together if you want.
4. Grill for a few minutes, or until a golden-brown crust has developed on the bottom. Avoid turning or checking too often since doing so can impede the caramelization process. Turn the pancakes with a large spatula and add extra oil.
5. Add half of the eggs, sausage, and cheese to the top after the bottom side has caramelized. To slightly compress it, gently push down.
6. Add the leftover hashbrowns on top. If desired, sprinkle more cheese on top and cook on a low-heat griddle.
7. Grill the cheese until it is totally melted. Serve right away!

Roasted Chickpeas with Herbs

Preparation time: **5 minutes**
Cooking time: **30 minutes**
Servings: **8**

Ingredients:
- ✓ 2 tbsp olive oil

- ✓ 1 tsp cumin
- ✓ 2 (15-oz) cans of low-salt chickpeas, drained & rinsed
- ✓ 1 tsp dried thyme

Directions:

1. Set the oven to 400°F. In a medium bowl, combine the chickpeas, cumin, olive oil, and thyme.
2. On a baking sheet, spread the chickpeas in a single layer. 30 minutes of roasting in the oven will make it crunchy on the exterior and creamy on the inside.
3. Serve right away.

Per serving: Calories: 165Kcal; Fat: 5.5g; Carbohydrates: 23g; Protein: 7g; Cholesterol: 0mg

Date Pumpkin Bites

Preparation time: 10 minutes
Cooking time: 20 minutes
Servings: 12 bites

Ingredients:
- ✓ 2 cups old-fashioned rolled oats
- ✓ ¾ cup pumpkin purée
- ✓ ¾ cup unsweetened applesauce
- ✓ 1 tsp coconut oil (for greasing)
- ✓ 1½ tsp nutmeg
- ✓ ½ cup coconut flakes
- ✓ ¾ cup dates, pitted & diced
- ✓ ¼ tsp ground cloves
- ✓ ¼ cup chopped apricots

Directions:

1. Set a muffin tray in the oven and preheat it to 350 degrees F. The oats should be blended into flour at this point.

2. Add the apricots, coconut flakes, nutmeg, cloves, and pumpkin purée to the applesauce. until smooth, process. Place the dates in and manually mix with a spoon.
3. Half-fill each cup in your muffin pan as you spoon the batter in, then bake for 18 to 20 minutes in the preheated oven.
4. Serve!

Per serving: Calories: 139Kcal; Fat: 6.1g; Carbohydrates: 23.6g; Protein: 5.4g; Cholesterol: 0mg

Marinated Berries

Preparation time: 10 minutes + marinating time

Cooking time: 0 minutes

Servings: 4

Ingredients:
- ✓ 2 cups fresh strawberries, hulled and quartered
- ✓ 1 cup fresh blueberries (optional)
- ✓ 2 tbsp sugar
- ✓ 1 tbsp balsamic vinegar
- ✓ 2 tbsp chopped fresh mint (optional)
- ✓ 1/8 tsp freshly ground black pepper

Directions:

1. In a large nonreactive dish, gently combine the strawberries, blueberries (if using), sugar, vinegar, mint (if using), and pepper.
2. Allow the flavors to mingle for a minimum of 25 minutes and a maximum of 2 hours. Serve.

Per serving: Calories: 73Kcal; Fat: 8g; Carbohydrates: 18g; Protein: 1g; Cholesterol: 0mg

Garlicky Kale Chips

Preparation time: 10 minutes
Cooking time: 15 minutes
Servings: 4

Ingredients:

- ✓ 1 bunch curly kale, remove tough stems & tear into big squares
- ✓ 2 tsp extra-virgin olive oil
- ✓ ¼ tsp kosher salt
- ✓ ¼ tsp garlic powder (optional)

Directions:

1. Set the oven's temperature to 325°F. Use parchment paper to cover your baking sheet with a rim.
2. Put the kale in a large bowl and add the oil. To thoroughly coat, massage for one to two minutes with your fingertips. On the baking sheet, spread it out.
3. Cook for 8 minutes, then thoroughly stir and cook for another 7 minutes, or until crispy. Add salt and, if desired, garlic powder. Serve.

Per serving: Calories: 28Kcal; Fat: 2g; Carbohydrates: 2g; Protein: 1g; Cholesterol: 0mg

Sesame-Garlic Edamame

Preparation time: 10 minutes
Cooking time: 3-5 minutes
Servings: 4

Ingredients:

- ✓ 1 (14-oz) package of frozen edamame in their shells
- ✓ 1 tbsp canola or sunflower oil
- ✓ 1 tbsp toasted sesame oil
- ✓ 3 garlic cloves, minced
- ✓ ½ tsp kosher salt
- ✓ ¼ tsp red pepper flakes (or more)

✓ Water, as needed

Directions:

1. Heat up a large saucepan of water to a rolling boil. Edamame are added and heated for 2 to 3 minutes in the cooking process. Drain well, then reserve.
2. In a large pan, heat the canola oil, sesame oil, garlic, salt, and red pepper flakes for one to two minutes.
3. Take the pan off the stove. Edamame should be added to the skillet and combined by stirring. Serve.

Per serving: Calories: 173Kcal; Fat: 12g; Carbohydrates: 8g; Protein: 11g; Cholesterol: 0mg

Spicy Guacamole

Preparation time: 10 minutes
Cooking time: 0 minutes
Servings: 4

Ingredients:
✓ 1 ripe avocado, peeled, pitted, & mashed
✓ 1½ tbsp freshly squeezed lime juice
✓ 1 tbsp minced jalapeño pepper, or to taste
✓ 1 tbsp minced red onion
✓ 1 tbsp chopped fresh cilantro
✓ 1 garlic clove, minced
✓ 1/8 tsp kosher salt
✓ Freshly ground black pepper to taste

Directions:

1. Combine the avocado, lime juice, jalapenos, onions, cilantro, garlic, salt, and pepper in a large bowl.
2. If preferred, serve with veggie sticks!

Per serving: Calories: 61Kcal; Fat: 5g; Carbohydrates: 4g; Protein: 1g; Cholesterol: 0mg

Blackberry-Thyme Granita

Preparation time: 10 minutes + freezing time

Cooking time: 0 minutes

Servings: 4

Ingredients:

- ✓ 4 cups fresh blackberries
- ✓ ¼ cup honey
- ✓ Juice of 1 lime
- ✓ 1 tbsp chopped fresh thyme

Directions:

1. Blend the blackberries, lime juice, honey, and thyme together in a blender.
2. Until smooth, blend. Using a fine-mesh strainer, pour the mixture into your bowl while pushing down to get the most juice out of it. Throw away the solids.
3. Fill a baking sheet measuring 9 by 13 inches with the ingredients.
4. Use a fork every 30 minutes to scrape the frozen liquid into a consistency like shaved ice throughout the four hours of freezing. Serve.

Per serving: Calories: 130Kcal; Fat: 1g; Carbohydrates: 32g; Protein: 2g; Cholesterol: 0mg

Easy Pear Bars

Preparation time: 25 minutes

Cooking time: 40 minutes

Servings: 1 dozen

Ingredients:

- ✓ ½ cup unsalted butter, melted

- ✓ 2 cups crushed sugar-free cookies
- ✓ ½ cup brown sugar
- ✓ 1 tsp. vanilla
- ✓ ½ cup unsweetened, flaked coconut
- ✓ 2 medium pears, cored and diced
- ✓ ⅓ cup flour
- ✓ ¼ tsp. baking powder
- ✓ ½ cup chopped dried apricots
- ✓ 2 eggs
- ✓ ½ tsp. ground ginger

Directions:

1. the oven to 350 degrees Fahrenheit. In a little mixing dish, combine the crumbled biscuits and the melted butter.
2. Press the mixture into a 9-inch square glass dish that has been lightly greased, then bake it for 20 minutes. After combining the flour, ginger, and baking powder, add the eggs, sugar, and vanilla to a separate bowl. The egg mixture is formed by vigorous stirring.
3. The pears, coconut, and apricots should then be added. After the biscuits have cooked for 20 minutes, evenly distribute the filling on top and continue baking until well browned.
4. After baking, remove the pan from the shelf and allow the cooked mixture to cool for 3–4 minutes before cutting it into strips. Enjoy!

Per serving: Calories: 2080Kcal; Fat: 111.8g; Carbohydrates: 241.32g; Protein: 35.93g; Cholesterol: 114mg

Homemade Peanut Butter Granola Bars

Preparation time: 15 minutes
Cooking time: 30 minutes
Servings: 8 bars

Ingredients:

- ✓ 2 cups whole rolled oats (not quick-cooking or instant)
- ✓ ½ cup smooth peanut butter
- ✓ ¼ cup 100% pure maple syrup
- ✓ ¼ cup brown rice syrup
- ✓ 1 tsp. pure vanilla extract
- ✓ ½ tsp. salt
- ✓ ½ tsp. ground cinnamon

Directions:

1. the oven to 350 degrees Fahrenheit. 10 by 10-inch parchment paper should be used to line an 8 by 8-inch baking sheet. In a small saucepan, combine the peanut butter, maple syrup, and brown rice syrup.
2. Just when the liquid is heated enough to dissolve the components and become smooth, reheat it gently over low heat while whisking with a fork. Get rid of the heat. The mixture should be slightly cooled down so that it is warm but not hot. Mix well after adding the cinnamon, oats, vanilla, and salt. Wet your hands, then firmly press the oats into the top of the pan to create the tightest-packing bars you can.
3. Bake the bars for 18 minutes, or until the edges are just beginning to brown. After the pan has finished baking, let it cool for approximately 10 minutes. By raising the parchment paper's corners, remove the bars from the pan. Place them on your cooling rack to finish cooling.
4. Make eight rectangles out of the bars using your 8-inch knife. Slice by applying pressure steadily in one motion.
5. Slice four times in the opposite direction after a single cut in the center.
6. The bars should be kept at room temperature in a container that is properly sealed.

Per serving: Calories: 208Kcal; Fat: 7.78g; Carbohydrates: 36.73g; Protein: 8.74g; Cholesterol: 30mg

Cherry Compote

Preparation time: 10 minutes
Cooking time: 30 minutes
Servings: 4

Ingredients:

- ✓ 2 peaches, pitted, halved
- ✓ 1 cup cherries, pitted
- ✓ ½ cup grape juice
- ✓ ½ cup strawberries
- ✓ 1 tablespoon liquid honey
- ✓ 1 teaspoon vanilla extract
- ✓ 1 teaspoon ground cinnamon

Directions:

1. Fill the pot with grape juice. Add cinnamon powder and vanilla essence.
2. Heat the liquid until it boils. After that, add strawberries, cherries, and peaches to the boiling grape juice. Add the liquid honey, then turn off the heat and cover the pot.
3. Give the compote 20 minutes to rest. Mix the compote well before placing it on a serving platter.

Per serving: Calories: 80Kcal; Fat: 0.3g; Carbohydrates: 19.1g; Protein: 1g; Cholesterol: 0mg

Grill Lemon Chicken

Preparation time: 10 minutes
Cooking time: 10 minutes
Servings: 6

Ingredients:

- ✓ 2 lbs. chicken breasts, boneless
- ✓ 1 tbsp lemon zest
- ✓ 2 tbsp fresh lemon juice

- ✓ 3 tbsp olive oil
- ✓ 1 tsp chili powder
- ✓ 1 tsp paprika
- ✓ ¼ cup fresh cilantro, chopped
- ✓ 1 tsp ground coriander
- ✓ Pepper
- ✓ Salt

Directions:

1. Put the chicken and the rest of the ingredients in the zip-top bag. Place the bag in the refrigerator for eight hours after sealing.
2. Cook the marinated chicken for 10 minutes on a hot grill.
3. Midway through, turn. Enjoy after serving.

Per serving: Calories: 354Kcal; Fat: 18.5g; Carbohydrates: 1.1g; Protein: 44g; Cholesterol: 135mg

Sweet & Tangy Chicken

Preparation time: 10 minutes
Cooking time: 6hours
Servings: 6

Ingredients:

- ✓ 2 lbs. chicken breasts, boneless
- ✓ 1 tsp garlic, minced
- ✓ 6 tbsp maple syrup
- ✓ ¼ cup olive oil
- ✓ 1 ¼ tsp Worcestershire sauce
- ✓ ½ cup Dijon mustard
- ✓ Pepper
- ✓ Salt

Directions:

1. Chicken should be put in the slow cooker. Pour the remaining ingredients over the chicken after mixing them.
2. Cook on low for 6 hours with the cover on. Use a fork to shred the chicken before serving.

Per serving: Calories: 439Kcal; Fat: 20.4g; Carbohydrates: 18.8g; Protein: 44.7g; Cholesterol: 135mg

Hearty Chicken Stew

Preparation time: 10 minutes
Cooking time: 6 hours
Servings: 6

Ingredients:
- ✓ 6 chicken thighs, boneless
- ✓ 2 cups chicken broth
- ✓ 1 ½ cups baby potatoes, cut in half
- ✓ 2 tomatoes, diced
- ✓ 1 tsp garlic, minced
- ✓ 1 small onion, diced
- ✓ 2 celery stalks, diced
- ✓ ¼ tsp chili powder
- ✓ 2 carrots, peeled& sliced
- ✓ Pepper
- ✓ Salt

Directions:

1. Put the chicken in the slow cooker, and then add the other ingredients.
2. Cook on low for 6 hours with the cover on. Use a fork to shred the chicken. Stir thoroughly, then plate.

Per serving: Calories: 308Kcal; Fat: 11.1g; Carbohydrates: 6.5g; Protein: 43.5g; Cholesterol: 130mg

Juicy Chicken Breast

Preparation time: 10 minutes
Cooking time: 6hours
Servings: 4

Ingredients:

- ✓ 1 lb. chicken breasts, boneless
- ✓ ¼ cup chicken broth
- ✓ 1 tbsp garlic, minced
- ✓ 1 ½ tbsp brown sugar
- ✓ ¼ cup red wine vinegar

Directions:

1. Put the chicken in the slow cooker. Over the chicken, pour the other ingredients.
2. Cook on low for 6 hours with the cover on. Enjoy after serving.

Per serving: Calories: 235Kcal; Fat: 8.5g; Carbohydrates: 4.2g; Protein: 33g; Cholesterol: 101mg

Juicy Chicken Patties

Preparation time: 10 minutes
Cooking time: 10 minutes
Servings: 12

Ingredients:

- ✓ 1 lb. ground chicken
- ✓ 2 tbsp olive oil
- ✓ ¼ tsp red pepper flakes
- ✓ 1 scallion, chopped
- ✓ 1 egg yolk
- ✓ Pepper
- ✓ Salt

Directions:

1. Chicken, red pepper flakes, scallions, egg yolk, pepper, and salt should all be well incorporated in a mixing bowl with the chicken.
2. In a pan, heat the oil to a medium-high temperature. From the chicken mixture, form little patties.
3. Patties should be cooked for two to three minutes on each side in heated oil.
4. Enjoy after serving.

Per serving: Calories: 97Kcal; Fat: 5.5g; Carbohydrates: 0.2g; Protein: 11.2g; Cholesterol: 51mg

Meatballs

Preparation time: 10 minutes
Cooking time: 16 minutes
Servings: 4

Ingredients:
- ✓ 1 egg
- ✓ 1 lb. ground chicken
- ✓ 2 tbsp Sriracha sauce
- ✓ 3/4 tsp chili powder
- ✓ 1/4 tsp paprika
- ✓ 1 tsp ground ginger
- ✓ 1 tsp garlic powder
- ✓ 1 oz parmesan cheese, shredded
- ✓ 1/4 cup almond flour
- ✓ Pepper
- ✓ Salt

Directions:

1. Your air fryer should be heated to 400 F. Chicken and the other ingredients should be combined thoroughly in a mixing basin.

2. The chicken mixture should be formed into equal-sized balls, which you should then cook in the air fryer basket for 16 minutes.
3. Midway through, turn. Enjoy after serving.

Per serving: Calories: 268Kcal; Fat: 11.8g; Carbohydrates: 2g; Protein: 36.9g; Cholesterol: 146mg

Italian Chicken Skewers

Preparation time: 10 minutes
Cooking time: 15 minutes
Servings: 6

Ingredients:

- ✓ 2 lbs. chicken breasts, boneless & cut into 1-inch pieces
- ✓ ½ tsp paprika
- ✓ 1 tbsp garlic, minced
- ✓ 2 tbsp lime juice
- ✓ ¼ cup olive oil
- ✓ 1 tsp rosemary, chopped
- ✓ 2 tsp dried oregano
- ✓ Pepper
- ✓ Salt

Directions:

1. Put the chicken and the rest of the ingredients in the zip-top bag. Place the bag in the refrigerator for eight hours after sealing.
2. After skewering the marinated chicken, roast it for 15 minutes over a hot grill. Midway through, turn. Enjoy after serving.

Per serving: Calories: 368Kcal; Fat: 19.7g; Carbohydrates: 2.3g; Protein: 44g; Cholesterol: 135mg

Savory Pork Chops

Preparation time: 10 minutes

Ingredients:

- ✓ 4 pork chops
- ✓ 3 tbsp maple syrup
- ✓ 1 ½ tsp cinnamon
- ✓ 2 tbsp butter
- ✓ 1 onion, sliced
- ✓ 3 apples, core & slice
- ✓ Pepper
- ✓ Salt

Directions:

1. Pork chops should be put in the slow cooker. Mix thoroughly after adding the additional ingredients to the pork chops.
2. Cook on low for 6 hours with the cover on. Stir thoroughly, then plate.

Per serving: Calories: 455Kcal; Fat: 26g; Carbohydrates: 39.4g; Protein: 18.9g; Cholesterol: 84mg

Perfect Beef

Preparation time: 10 minutes

Cooking time: 6hours

Servings: 6

Ingredients:

- ✓ 3 lbs. beef roast
- ✓ 1 tbsp maple syrup
- ✓ 1 tbsp garlic, minced
- ✓ 1 small onion, sliced
- ✓ oz can green chilies
- ✓ 14 oz can tomato, crushed

- ✓ 1 tbsp olive oil
- ✓ ¼ tsp cayenne pepper
- ✓ ½ tsp cumin powder
- ✓ 1 tsp thyme
- ✓ 1 tsp onion powder
- ✓ 1 tsp garlic powder
- ✓ 1 tbsp chili powder
- ✓ 1 tbsp smoked paprika
- ✓ Pepper
- ✓ Salt

Directions:

1. In the slow cooker, put the tomato, maple syrup, garlic, onion, chilies, pepper, and salt.
2. Rub meat with a mixture of oil, cayenne, cumin, thyme, garlic powder, chili powder, smoked paprika, pepper, and salt. Meat should be put in the slow cooker.
3. Cook on low for 6 hours with the cover on. Use a fork to shred the meat before serving.

Per serving: Calories: 488Kcal; Fat: 16.9g; Carbohydrates: 10.8g; Protein: 70.3g; Cholesterol: 203mg

Delicious Pork Carnitas

Preparation time: 10 minutes
Cooking time: 8 hours
Servings: 12

Ingredients:

- ✓ 5 lbs. pork roast
- ✓ 1 cup orange juice
- ✓ 1 tbsp garlic, minced
- ✓ 1 medium onion, sliced
- ✓ 2 tbsp olive oil

- ✓ 1 ½ tsp ground coriander
- ✓ 1 tbsp dried thyme
- ✓ Pepper
- ✓ Salt

Directions:

1. Rub the pork roast with a mixture of thyme, ground coriander, pepper, salt, and other seasonings. Put the slow cooker's pork roast in there.
2. Over the pig roast, add the other ingredients. Cook on low for 8 hours with the cover on. Use a fork to shred the meat before serving.

Per serving: Calories: 427Kcal; Fat: 20.3g; Carbohydrates: 3.6g; Protein: 54.2g; Cholesterol: 163mg

Healthy Sweet Potato Crab Cakes

Preparation time: 15 minutes, plus 30 minutes to chill

Cooking time: 40 minutes

Servings: 4

Ingredients:

FOR THE SAUCE

- ✓ ⅔ cup nonfat plain Greek yogurt
- ✓ 2 tbsps. chopped fresh parsley
- ✓ 2 tbsps. chopped fresh basil
- ✓ 2 tbsps. fresh lemon juice
- ✓ 1 garlic clove, minced

FOR THE CRAB CAKES

- ✓ 2 tbsps. extra-virgin olive oil, divided
- ✓ 1 pound lump crabmeat
- ✓ 2 large sweet potatoes, peeled and halved
- ✓ 1 tbsp. nonfat plain Greek yogurt
- ✓ 1 large egg

- ✓ ¼ tsp. freshly ground black pepper
- ✓ ¼ tsp. dried thyme
- ✓ ¼ cup chopped fresh parsley
- ✓ ¼ cup chopped red onion
- ✓ ½ cup dried unseasoned bread crumbs
- ✓ 4 lemon wedges (optional)

Directions:

TO MAKE THE SAUCE

1. In a small bowl, thoroughly blend the yogurt, basil, parsley, lemon juice, and garlic. Among the four tiny storage containers, divide the sauce.

TO MAKE THE CRAB CAKES

2. Your medium saucepan of water has to come to a boil. After adding them, boil the sweet potatoes for 15 to 20 minutes, or until tender. Place in a bowl and let it cool. Sweet potatoes should be mashed. Mix thoroughly before adding the yogurt, pepper, thyme, parsley, and onion.
3. Mix in the crabmeat and breadcrumbs. Lastly, combine thoroughly after adding the egg. Set on a dish after being gently formed into 8 cakes. To get a beautiful setting, refrigerate for 30 minutes. 1 tablespoon of oil should be heated over medium heat in a cast-iron or nonstick pan. Four crab cakes should be added and cooked for a total of approximately 8 minutes, flipping once, or until browned on both sides.
4. Repeat, and then put two crab cakes in each of the four containers for storage.
5. Reheat the crab cakes and dish them with the sauce and lemon wedges (if using) when you are ready to serve.

Per serving: Calories: 319Kcal; Fat: 10g; Carbohydrates: 30g; Protein: 28g; Cholesterol: 46mg

Basil & Tomato Egg Bites

Servings'
Cooking Timex

Ingredients:

- ✓ Eggs, about 6 Medium
- ✓ 300 g Heavy cream, and/or cottage cheese
- ✓ 3 g Salt, plus more to taste
- ✓ Cherry tomatoes, optional, as needed
- ✓ Pine nuts, optional, as needed
- ✓ Finishing oil, such as high-quality extra-virgin olive oil, optional, as needed
- ✓ Basil, fresh leaves, optional, as needed
- ✓ Black pepper, optional, as needed
- ✓ Equipment
- ✓ 6-4oz mason jars

Directions:

1. Make a water bath that is 185 degrees Fahrenheit ready. Combine the cream and a few eggs in a mixer. Blend it on medium speed for a while to get it nice and silky. The egg foundation should be poured into the jars all the way to the very last notch.
2. Twist the lid of each Mason jar until it is secure but still easily opened with a fingertip.
3. The vents allow air to escape when the jars are immersed in water. If the jars are sealed too firmly, the pressure from the air inside might force them to break. In the water bath, place the jars and cook for 25 minutes.
4. Remove them from the water bath after they are cooked. Cut the cherry tomatoes in half or quarters. Sliced tomatoes and pine nuts should be combined in a small dish along with some olive

oil. Before spooning the mixture on top of your egg bits, season them with salt and pepper. Serve

Deviled Eggs

Servings'

Cooking Timex

Ingredients:

- ✓ 12 Eggs
- ✓ Ice water, for ice bath, as needed
- ✓ 6 oz Crème fraîche, or sour cream
- ✓ 56 oz Dijon mustard
- ✓ 07 oz Kosher salt
- ✓ 02 oz Black pepper
- ✓ Smoked paprika, optional, to garnish, as needed
- ✓ Herbs, fresh as needed

Directions:

1. Warm up the water bath to 194 °F. Add the eggs with caution after the water has reached the right temperature. Twenty minutes to get ready.
2. Make an ice bath. As soon as the eggs are finished frying, they should be carefully moved from the saucepan to the ice bath. To give the tastes a chance to mingle, a 30-minute delay is advised. Gently take each egg from the cold water one at a time, then gently break and peel the shell. Transferring the meal to a new dish is necessary.
3. Continue peeling eggs until all of them are done. Each egg should be carefully split into two equal halves. Transfer the yolks to a clean dish as you go. The cooked yolks and the other ingredients should be combined in the pitcher of a food processor to produce the filling. Process until smooth, pausing to stir

occasionally to maintain the appropriate consistency. Spoon the mixture into a piping bag and refrigerate it after it has achieved the required consistency.

4. Your egg whites should be arranged on a serving dish. Carefully pipe the liquid into each one to fill them. Until you are ready to serve, cover the eggs and chill them in the refrigerator. Garnish and serve.

5. Dust the paprika and a few sprigs of fresh herbs on just before serving using a fine-mesh sieve or your fingers.

Egg Cups

Servings'

Cooking Timex

Ingredients:

- ✓ For the Egg Mixture
- ✓ 2 cup cottage cheese
- ✓ 8 eggs lightly beaten
- ✓ 1 cup almond flour
- ✓ 2 tsp. baking powder
- ✓ 1/2 tsp. kosher salt
- ✓ For the Filling
- ✓ 8 ounces ham diced
- ✓ 1 cup cheddar cheese shredded
- ✓ 4 green onions sliced
- ✓ 1/2 cup diced mushrooms sautéed
- ✓ 1 tsp. fresh Thyme
- ✓ 1 tbsp. all purpose flour

Directions:

1. For a bath, raise the water's temperature to 167 degrees Fahrenheit. In a blender, combine the cottage cheese, eggs,

almond flour, baking soda, and kosher salt. Blend until well combined.

2. Blend everything together in a blender until it's smooth. Combine the ham, cheddar cheese, green onions, chopped mushrooms, thyme, and all-purpose flour in a separate bowl. Put a 4-ounce canning jar with half of the egg mixture inside. Fill jars no more than 3/4 full with the egg mixture after adding two tablespoons of the filling and spreading it evenly.

3. With your fingers, put on the caps. Cook in a water bath for an hour with the jars submerged. Take them out of the water when the timer goes off.

4. You may either eat it directly from the jar or put it on a platter.

Blackberry Lemon Martini

Time to prepare: 20 minutes

Time to Cook: 3 hours

Servings: 8

Ingredients:
- ✓ 2 cups frozen blackberries
- ✓ 2 cups vodka
- ✓ 1/2 cup lemon juice
- ✓ 1/4 cup superfine sugar

Instructions:

1. At 135 degrees Fahrenheit, the sous vide water bath should be ready for use.

2. The fruit and vodka should be combined in a mason jar. Cover the container loosely. For three hours, cook the Mason jar in the sous vide bath.

3. Once the food has finished cooking, pour the cooking liquid into a glass.

4. In a cocktail shaker, combine blackberry vodka, sugar, lemon juice, and ice. Serve.

Nutrition: Calories 171 |Total Fat 0.3g |Saturated Fat 0.1g |Carbohydrate 10g | Dietary Fiber 2g | Sugars 8.3g | Protein 0.6g

Rosemary-Lemon Vodka

Time to prepare: 10 minutes

Time to Cook: 3 hours

Servings: 16

Ingredients:
- ✓ 1 (750 mL) bottle vodka
- ✓ Zest of 6 lemons, sliced
- ✓ 6 sprigs fresh rosemary, chopped

Directions

1. The water bath for sous vide cooking has to be prepared and heated to 145 degrees F.
2. Add each of the rosemary vodka's components to a zipper-lock bag. Apply the water immersion technique to the bag's zip-lock closure.
3. In the sous vide bath, cook the sealed bag for three hours. Pour the liquid into a basin once the cooking is complete.
4. Serve after an overnight cold.

Nutrition: Calories 110 | Total Fat 0.1g | Saturated Fat 0g | Carbohydrate 2.3g | Dietary Fiber 0.8g | Sugars 0.5g | Protein 0.3g

Limoncello

Time to prepare: 10 minutes

Time to Cook: 2 hours

Servings: 12

Ingredients:
- ✓ 10 fresh lemons, sliced
- ✓ 4 cups vodka
- ✓ 4 cups water

✓ 1 ½ cups sugar

Directions

1. The temperature of the sous vide water bath should be set at 135 degrees F. Zip-top bag with vodka and lemon in it.
2. Apply the water immersion technique to the bag's zip-lock closure. In the sous vide bath with the sealed bag, cook for two hours.
3. Pour the boiled liquid into a basin after it is completed. Water and sugar should be well mixed in a saucepan. Add the lemon vodka to the sugar syrup and carefully combine.
4. Serve after an overnight cold.

Nutrition: Calories 279 | Total Fat 0.1g | Saturated Fat 0g | Carbohydrate 29.5g | Dietary Fiber 1.4g | Sugars 26.2g | Protein 0.5g

Bacon-Infused Vodka

Time to prepare: 20 minutes

Time to Cook: 45 minutes

Servings: 8

Ingredients:
✓ 2 cups vodka
✓ 8 oz. bacon
✓ 3 tbsp bacon grease

Directions

1. The water bath for sous vide cooking has to be prepared and heated to 150 degrees F.
2. The bacon should be crisp after 16 minutes of baking at 400 degrees F. When the bacon has had time to cool, transfer it to a zip-lock bag.
3. Combine the ingredients for bacon vodka in a zip-lock bag.

4. Apply the water immersion technique to the bag's zip-lock closure. In the sous vide bath, cook the sealed bag for 45 minutes.
5. Pour the boiled liquid into a basin after it is completed. Serve after an overnight cold.

Nutrition: Calories 298 | Total Fat 13.6g | Saturated Fat 4.6g | Carbohydrate 0.4g | Dietary Fiber 0g | Sugars 0g | Protein 10.5g

Eggnog

Time to prepare: 10 minutes

Time to Cook: 1 hour

Servings: 8

Ingredients:

- ✓ 6 large eggs
- ✓ 1 quart milk
- ✓ 1 cup heavy cream
- ✓ 1/2 cup bourbon
- ✓ 1/2 cup brandy
- ✓ 1/2 cup sugar
- ✓ 1 tsp vanilla bean paste
- ✓ 1/2 tsp ground nutmeg
- ✓ 1/2 tsp ground cinnamon
- ✓ 1 pinch of salt

Directions

1. The water bath for sous vide cooking has to be prepared and heated to 144 degrees F.
2. The components for the eggnog should be blended in a blender until totally smooth. The eggnog mixture should be placed in a zip-lock bag.
3. Apply the water immersion technique to the bag's zip-lock closure. In the sous vide bath, cook the sealed bag for one hour.

4. When done, transfer the liquid into a basin. Serve after an overnight cold.

Nutrition: Calories 252 | Total Fat 11.8g | Saturated Fat 6.2g | Carbohydrate 20g| Dietary Fiber 0.1g | Sugars 19g | Protein 9.1g

Spiced Mulled Wine

Time to prepare: 10 minutes

Time to Cook: 1 hour

Servings: 4

Ingredients:
- ✓ 1 bottle red wine
- ✓ 1/2 tsp allspice powder
- ✓ 2 cups orange juice
- ✓ 2 tbsp orange juice
- ✓ 2 cinnamon sticks
- ✓ 2 tsp brown sugar
- ✓ 1 vanilla pod, sliced
- ✓ 2-star anise

Directions

1. The water bath for sous vide cooking has to be prepared and heated to 140 degrees F.
2. Put each wine component in its own zip-lock bag. Apply the water immersion technique to the bag's zip-lock closure. In the sous vide bath, cook the sealed bag for one hour.
3. Pour the boiled liquid into a basin after it is completed. Serve after an overnight cold.

Nutrition: Calories 150| Total Fat 0.3g | Saturated Fat 0.1g | Carbohydrate 18.1g |Dietary Fiber 0.9g | Sugars 12.7g |Protein 1g

Maple Drambuie

Time to prepare: 15 minutes

Time to Cook: 30 minutes

Servings: 2

Ingredients:
- ✓ 1/2 cup scotch whiskey
- ✓ 1/4 cup water
- ✓ 2 tbsp maple syrup
- ✓ 1 tsp fresh rosemary leaves, chopped
- ✓ 1 tsp whole fennel seeds

Directions

1. It should be prepared and cooked to 180 degrees F for the sous vide water bath.
2. Place all of the Drambuie ingredients in a zip-lock bag.
3. Apply the water immersion technique to the bag's zip-lock closure. In the sous vide bath, cook the sealed bag for 30 minutes.
4. Pour the boiled liquid into a basin after it is completed. Serve after an overnight cold.

Nutrition: Calories 143 | Total Fat 0.6g | Saturated Fat 0.1g | Carbohydrate 15.3g |Dietary Fiber 1.3g | Sugars 11.9g | Protein 0.5g

Hot Spiced Cider

Time to prepare: 10 minutes

Time to Cook: 1 hour

Servings: 2

Ingredients:
- ✓ 2 cups apple cider
- ✓ 1 tsp cinnamon ground
- ✓ 1/2 tbsp honey
- ✓ 1/4 tsp black peppercorns
- ✓ 1 tbsp orange juice
- ✓ 2 orange slices

Directions

1. The water bath for sous vide cooking has to be prepared and heated to 140 degrees F.
2. Add all the ingredients for the cider to a zip-lock bag. Apply the water immersion technique to the bag's zip-lock closure. In the sous vide bath, cook the sealed bag for one hour.
3. Pour the boiled liquid into a basin after it is completed.
4. Serve after an overnight cold.

Nutrition: Calories 142 Total Fat 0.3g Saturated Fat 0g Carbohydrate 32g Dietary Fiber 1.2g Sugars 28g Protein 0.4g

Bacon-Infused Bourbon

Time to prepare: 10 minutes

Time to Cook: 1 hour

Servings: 8

Ingredients:
- ✓ 2 cups bourbon
- ✓ 8 oz. smoked bacon, cooked
- ✓ 3 tbsp bacon fat
- ✓ 3 tbsp brown sugar

Directions:

1. The water bath for sous vide cooking has to be prepared and heated to 150 degrees F.
2. Put each bourbon ingredient in a zip-lock bag. Apply the water immersion technique to the bag's zip-lock closure. In the sous vide bath, cook the sealed bag for one hour.
3. After everything is ready, drain the hot mixture into a basin while the bourbon cools.
4. Serve after an overnight cold.

Nutrition: Calories 295 | Total Fat 12.5g |Saturated Fat 4.1g | Carbohydrate 3.7g| Dietary Fiber 0g | Sugars 3.3g | Protein 10.5g

Berry Mixed Bourbon

Time to prepare: 10 minutes

Time to Cook: 2 hours

Servings: 4

Ingredients:
- ✓ 1/2 lb. raspberries, halved
- ✓ 1/2 lb. blueberries, halved
- ✓ 1 ½ cup bourbon

Directions

1. The temperature of the sous vide water bath should be set at 135 degrees F.
2. Put each bourbon ingredient in a zip-lock bag. Apply the water immersion technique to the bag's zip-lock closure.
3. In the sous vide bath with the sealed bag, cook for two hours.
4. Pour the boiled liquid into a basin after it is completed.
5. Serve after an overnight cold.

Nutrition: Calories 255 |Total Fat 0.6g | Saturated Fat 0g | Carbohydrate 15g |Dietary Fiber 5.1g | Sugars 8.1g | Protein 1.1g

Vanilla Coffee

Time to prepare: 10 minutes

Time to Cook: 3 hours

Servings: 6

Ingredients:
- ✓ 3 cups water
- ✓ 32 oz. strong black coffee
- ✓ 1 cup sugar
- ✓ 1/2 cup coffee beans

✓ 2 vanilla beans, split

Directions:

1. The water bath for sous vide cooking has to be prepared and heated to 145 degrees F.
2. Put each coffee ingredient in its own zip-lock bag. Apply the water immersion technique to the bag's zip-lock closure. In the sous vide bath, cook the sealed bag for three hours
3. Pour the boiled liquid into a basin after it is completed.
4. Serve after an overnight cold.

Nutrition: Calories 127 |Total Fat 0g | Saturated Fat 0g | Carbohydrate 33.4g |Dietary Fiber 0g | Sugars 33.3g | Protein 0.2g

CONCLUSION

Congratulations! The unofficial TikTok Cookbook has come to an end after taking you on a gastronomic trip through the intriguing world of popular food trends and viral dishes on TikTok. We have examined a wide range of delectable recipes, inventive cooking methods, and the contagious love of food that pervades the TikTok community throughout this book. The way we find, make, and share recipes has been changed by TikTok, from the famed feta spaghetti to the notorious cloud bread. It has developed into a venue where amateur cooks, food aficionados, and professional chefs may mingle to display their culinary skills and try out novel tastes. You have probably learned about the influence of social media on the development of our culinary culture as you have read through this cookbook. TikTok has given regular people a voice, enabling them to motivate millions of others with their simple yet delectable recipes. It has also generated a surge of culinary creativity, inspiring chefs to push the envelope, modify tried-and-true dishes, and add their own special spins. Beyond the viral hits and cutting-edge cuisine, though, TikTok has bonded people through the enjoyment of a common pastime. Through their shared love of cooking and eating, it has helped to build a sense of community among people from all over the globe. We are reminded that we are all connected by our fundamental need for nutrition and our desire to relish the flavors of life by TikTok's demonstration that food has the power to transcend language barriers, cultural differences, and geographic distances. We want you to take everything you've learned from the TikTok community and use it in your own kitchen as you wrap up your culinary journey. Don't be scared to let your originality show; embrace the pleasure of cooking and the spirit of exploration. TikTok recipes are beautiful not just because they taste well but also because they let you customize them as you choose. Keep in mind that the kitchen is your canvas and that cooking is an art form. The recipes and methods you have learned here may be used as a starting point for unlimited culinary research, regardless of whether you are an experienced chef or a novice cook. So go ahead and prepare your ingredients, start your camera, and show the world your own TikTok-worthy masterpieces. We appreciate your participation as we explore the unofficial TikTok Cookbook. We hope it has motivated you to try new culinary experiences, unearth abilities, and find delight in the simple act of cooking and dining with others. May your kitchen always be a place of joy, love, and, of course, the mouthwatering fragrances of the meals that make TikTok a foodie's dream come true. Happy TikTok Ing and cooking!

Made in the USA
Monee, IL
01 December 2023

47852462R00072